In Heaven
There Are
No Thunderstorms

Celebrating the Liturgy with Developmentally Disabled People

Gijs Okhuijsen, O.M.I.
Cees van Opzeeland

Translated by
G. P. A. van Daelen

Foreword by
Henri J. M. Nouwen

A Liturgical Press Book

THE LITURGICAL PRESS
Collegeville, Minnesota

Cover design by Fred Petters

1   2   3   4   5   6   7   8   9   10

Library of Congress Cataloging-in-Publication Data

Okhuisjen, Gijs.
    [In de hemel onweert het niet. English]
    In heaven there are no thunderstorms : celebrating the liturgy with developmentally disabled people / Gijs Okhuisjen and Cees van Opzeeland ; translated by G.P.A. van Daelen ; foreword by Henri J. M. Nouwen.
        p.   cm.
    Translation of: In de hemel onweert het niet.
    ISBN 0-8146-1999-1
    1. Catholic Church and the mentally handicapped.   2. Mentally handicapped—Religious life.   3. Liturgical adaptation—Catholic Church.   4. Worship programs.   I. Opzeeland, Cees van.   II. Title.
BX2347.8.M4038   1992
264'.02'00874—dc20   91-44407
                                                                            CIP

Contents

Foreword

This book could have been called "The Gospel Rediscovered." Gijs Okhuijsen and Cees van Opzeeland have rediscovered the gospel for themselves and others in their life and work with women and men with a mental handicap. I am grateful that their stories about this rediscovery have made it from Holland to the United States and can now be read by many who do not know Dutch.

My own life with mentally handicapped people in the L'Arche community, Daybreak, in Toronto, strongly confirms the experiences this book describes. It is, first of all, the experience that those who cannot read, speak, or write in the way most others can offer us the unique opportunity to express our strongest conviction and deepest feeling in a way that comes right from the heart and goes right to the heart. But it also is the experience that those who call us to speak from the heart to heart become, themselves, witnesses to us of the good news. Thus the very people to whom we are sent become our guides. This is the great and beautiful mystery of the mutuality of true ministry which is so directly visible among those who are "poor in spirit."

This wonderful, joyful, playful book shows how those who may be marginal in the eyes of our society stand in the center of the good news. They say to us, "Tell us the good news, tell it simply, tell it directly, tell it with your whole being, tell it without hesitations, ambiguities, or subtleties, tell it so we can see it, hear it, taste it, touch it, and thus know it with our heart." They also say, "Listen to the good news that comes from our hearts, even when we do not have words. Receive the love and the gratitude hidden in our poverty and brokenness and dare to believe that the little people to whom you want to show God's love also have God's love to show to you."

Ever since I have been sharing my life with mentally handicapped people, I can no longer hide the good news behind my intelligence or rhetorical talents. I am too quickly unmasked! When there is something sad to be told there are tears, when there is something joyful to announce there are smiles. When I am boring, I know it directly. When I am inspiring, I know that, too. Those who can speak don't wait until after the service to say it, and those who can walk don't hesitate to walk away or to come closer when they feel like it. This book shows the great mystery that the "poor in spirit" call us to truly celebrate the love of God.

It is obvious that Gijs Okhuijsen and Cees van Opzeeland have written down their spiritual adventure to offer support and guidance to all who look for appropriate liturgical forms in their pastoral work with mentally handicapped people. But, as I read their book, I kept saying to myself, "But, aren't the handicapped people calling far beyond their own circle? Aren't they calling us to minister from heart to heart and to trust even more in the mutuality of that ministry?"

I am increasingly convinced that the very simple, but demanding, love of Jesus is news from the poor to the poor. We can speak it from that place in our hearts where we are most vulnerable, most wounded, yes, most handicapped. But it is in that very place, too, where we can hear it and let it bear fruit. Jesus did not say, "Blessed are those who care for the poor," but "Blessed are the poor." We all are poor. It is precisely in our poverty that we need to speak and hear the words of healing. This book certainly shows the way.

Henri J. M. Nouwen

Preface

It is ten years ago now that Cees van Opzeeland, a former student of mine and one of the coauthors of this collection, was ordained a deacon by Bishop T. Zwartkruis. The ordination took place in the chapel of the institution where he was working at the time. This ceremony was in many respects a moving experience. The way the bishop laid on his hands and went through the other ordination rites, seriously and cordially, was impressive. Even more striking was the way the residents who were present reacted. They expressed their joy without being inhibited by social rules. One of them, for instance, kissed the wife of the newly ordained deacon on her mouth.

The fact that people with mental retardation also live among us brings us face to face with the incompleteness of our own existence. Parents, in particular, have this experience. But for such persons themselves, being mentally disabled is often and in many respects very painful. They experience much, but time after time they are threatened to be drowned by their feelings, perhaps to become chaotic. They often lack the instruments to express their experiences, causing them to be locked up with them in an isolated and puzzling darkness. During the postwar period the insights and skills of how to help people with mental retardation increased considerably. Still, very often the skeptical question has been raised as to whether there is any sense in trying to instill into these damaged brains and simple hearts some awareness of God's caring presence.

This selection of liturgical services by Cees van Opzeeland and Gijs Okhuijsen will give you an opportunity to become acquainted with a well-thought-out and creative approach and will enable you at the same time to see how this mentally retarded part of God's people is reacting to this approach. These pastors and their parishioners have been a new revelation to me. I mean this in a very literal sense: They have made me aware—I say this deliberately—of the mysteries of God, who says: "I am on your side."

I am convinced that in dealing with people who are mentally retarded, forms of authentic faith can be found. Moreover, I feel that it is a pastoral art—in the real sense of the word—to celebrate the liturgy in such a way that these people are enabled to express and exchange their religious experiences with each other and their pastor. The need for such a specialized pastoral care was first realized in the United States. In my book *On the Way to an Empirical Spiritual Care,** I gave an account of my introduction to this kind of pastoral care during a service conducted by Reverend Perske, a minister in Topeka, Kansas.

It was during his stay with Reverend Perske that Cees van Opzeeland, among other things, learned a lot about this art. Thanks to the creative cooperation of our authors, this art has been further developed and refined. The collection offered here is a reflection of the results of this cooperation.

This book will help every pastor to learn about his profession. For it is in celebrating together with these faithful that the deepest elements of liturgical action reveal themselves: the harmony of feelings, the reciprocity of the relations between pastor and parishioners, the learning and healing that happens together. In other words, everyone participating becomes enriched by all.

*W. J. Berger, *Op weg naar een empirische zielzorg* (Utrecht: Dekker and V. D. Vegt, 1965) 69.

At any rate, without the dedicated and intelligent contributions of the professional staffs of these institutions, celebrations like these would never have been possible. From the existing conditions, they give form to these liturgical experiments as formulated by the American bishops and as they represent the universal Church.

I say this very cautiously. Perhaps they themselves would say: "We wouldn't do all this if it were not for these residents." If that is the case, I joyfully feel that the joy of these "little ones" has become a revelation for men and women of learning and intelligence.

W. J. Berger, Ph.D.

Introduction

On World Pet's Day—just to mention one feast—the residents of our institutions bring their "pets" to the chapel. For one, it might be a picture of his mother, who passed away. Another might bring a present she got. A third, a drawing—a present for the pastor. They bring along whatever keeps them busy, or else they just talk about it. They come into the house of God their Father just the way they are.

The pastor prepares the liturgy; the residents bring life as it is. The pastor, as narrator of God's dealings with people, must tell his stories in such a way that the residents are able to identify with them. And every week brings once again the surprising experience of seeing how the Bible story and one of the residents come together.

Our residents don't reason about liturgy, they live it. They play, celebrate, pray, sing, and share bread. When they like something they applaud, yawn when it is boring, and become unruly when the pastor misses the boat. They interrupt his sermon, ask questions, or discuss the topic at hand. They sense whether our prayer is real, and only in that case will they repeat the words. And at Holy Communion they may kiss the pastor spontaneously. They are in charge!

A sermon must never be complicated or difficult. Mental retardation forces us to share God's message in forms as simple and crisp as possible. But because of this, the biblical message is experienced as a personal reality. We have to do our utmost and use all our imagination to express this reality in forms mentally retarded people are able to grasp.

This collection contains twenty-five narrative descriptions of this liturgical adventure. They all have this in common: We pastors enjoyed them thoroughly. The selection is from celebrations held over a period of two years at Huize Ursula and De Hartekamp, both institutions for people with mental retardation. In the selection are celebrations of the Eucharist as well as Communion services. They came about with the help of many enthusiastic fellow workers, who accepted the challenge of celebrating the faith with the residents of our institutions.

The mentally retarded people in these stories prove to be genuinely believing people who deserve to be accepted as full members of the Church, and whose often unique expressions of faith have to be taken seriously. We have personally experienced our institutions to be places of faith and of faithful celebrations. We pass on our experiences to you. Perhaps they will become an inspiration somewhere else.

G. J. Okhuijsen, O.M.I.
Huize Ursula, Nieuwveen

C. J. J. M. van Opzeeland
De Hartekamp, Heemstede

Part I
The Liturgical Year

A Sunday in Advent:
"Gé and Cora should go to the river"

Preparation

In the celebration of the Second Sunday of Advent we pay attention to John the Baptist. The group leaders of the various sections are asked to read, or preferably to tell in their own words, the story of John. The text presented below might serve as a guide for others.

We ask the leaders to discuss with the residents these questions: What would we want to rid ourselves of? What would we like to throw into the river so that we might become a little bit renewed again? The answers are to be written on strips of blue paper to be brought along to the chapel on Sunday.

The Liturgy

On that Sunday we heave a sigh of relief when we notice that one of the residents enthusiastically waves his "blue wave" as he enters the chapel. Apparently he likes what he has thought of. And fortunately, one or two more residents have something to be gotten rid of. The preparation has paid off!

After the opening song and prayer, we light the second candle of our Advent wreath, our countdown calendar on the way to Christmas. The wreath is large and hangs high up in the center of the chapel, which is why it always takes a lot of time and effort to get it to burn. Everyone watches the operation breathlessly. And when the candle finally burns, a spontaneous, resounding applause goes up.

Together we sing about this second candle:

> The time has come, it's Advent again,
> Look, the second candle starts burning,
> A song about light, a song you know,
> Let it be heard, begin the song.
> What a joy—sing it aloud,
> Little light, never never go out.
>
> (A. Bosch and J. Stokkermans, *Je hoort wel eens zeggen*)

After the song the pastor walks over to the flannel board and explains: "Here you see a big river and next to it John, inviting people to make a fresh start. Now, who are the ones around him? Let's see. That one over there . . . that one is a thief, a moneygrubber, one who only thinks of me, me, me. And that one over there? . . . That's a soldier. He prefers war rather than peace. This one here? He wants to play the boss. That's clear! He is walking around sticking his nose in the air. Many don't take the slightest notice of John. Or they laugh at him. But there are some who return. John tells them to change their lives. He calls them 'to convert,' 'to change,' 'to become new.' How to go about that? John says: 'Come to the river. I'll baptize you and thus everything, all filth and nastiness, all trouble and grief, will be washed off. All of it will be washed away in the water so that all of you will emerge fresh and renewed again.'

"Some of John's listeners step down into the river. Watch!" The pastor puts small figures into the flannel-board water of the Jordan. "These people really want to try to become new people. Advent is such a time to start all over again. That's why we told you John's story. If we followed John's advice, what would we want to wash off in the river?"

Gerard comes forward. Apparently, he has waited a long time for this moment. Representing his group, he has brought a blue strip, cut like waves. On it is written the line "pests and quarrelsome fellows." Together, he and the buddies in his section came up with this idea, and the attendant wrote it on the strip for them. Gerard has difficulty walking, and climbing the altar steps carrying his cardboard "wave" is very hard for him. Don't worry! He just sits down and goes up backward, one step at a time, to drop his group's "trash" into the River Jordan. There, his blue strip is stuck onto the river—the "pests and quarrelsome fellows" are committed to the waves. The pastor helps Gerard get back to his place. Then two other groups carry their "trash" to the river. No throngs, though. For a moment, there is an embarrassing silence.

Obviously, something is bugging some of them. Is it because they did not prepare anything in their section? Or was the question too blunt, not tactful enough? The pastor just has to come up with some other things that should be washed off. He offers some examples and receives some help from the residents. But not much! Has it perhaps been too difficult?

Suddenly Theo steps forward. He has great difficulty speaking; still, he wants to say something. The pastor can hardly understand him. He catches something like "cola" but doesn't know what to do with it. Theo tries again. The fact that the pastor can't understand him is clearly getting on his nerves. But still the pastor can't figure it out. He manages to carry it off by saying, "So that should also be thrown into the river?" Theo accepts this. The pastor throws the "unknown" into the river, and Theo returns to his place.

Pleased that he saved himself from a difficult situation so well, the pastor starts praying. We pray that we ourselves may become new during the Advent season.

After the celebration Gé tells a section leader that he was glad the pastor could not understand Theo. That morning Gé had had quite a collision with Cora, one of the leaders. The residents experienced the incident as a real row. "Cola" turned out to be "Cora." Gé and Cora should go to the river to wash off their argument. For Theo, this was the logical consequence of the story. He had understood the message quite well. Gé and Cora, too?

A Story About John the Baptist

"His name was John, and he lived in Israel. He was quite familiar with the prophet Isaiah's stories about God, who would himself send a Savior. John liked to listen to these stories. After all, he was a born storyteller himself. His calling was to baptize. That's why he was called John the Baptist.

"John told the people that this time God would send a real Savior. This one would not be, as they might think, like the other kings. After all, all those kings, except David, had been bunglers.

"As long as the real Savior hadn't arrived yet, people could prepare themselves for his arrival. They should stop saying nothing but I, I, I. Neither should they keep on walking around sticking their noses in the air and playing the boss with each other, causing only grief and a lot of loneliness. Those who accepted John's preaching were baptized. Not in a baptismal font in a church, but in the open, in the water of a river with lots of people around. And those who were baptized left all their troubles and grief behind in the water and emerged fresh, as if they had been reborn.

"One day John was talking and baptizing again when a man approached him saying, 'John, I want you to baptize me!' Immediately John saw that this man was Jesus, his cousin. He had always thought that Jesus was special. The way he talked and acted, he seemed exactly like the real Savior of God that Isaiah had talked about. And John told the people who were standing around him, 'Look, there he is! That's the Savior who has been promised by God. He is called Jesus.' And talking to Jesus, John said, 'You want me to baptize you? That's out of the question!'

"But Jesus had already stepped down into the water. He didn't think himself superior to going down into the water in which people had left behind their troubles and sins. After all, he didn't want to be their king or boss but a real Savior, a comforter and a friend.

"Even John was surprised that Jesus wanted to be that kind of a Savior. He was amazed and baptized Jesus as he had asked.

"And God himself let the people know: 'This is my Son and your Savior. I love him and he—in turn—loves all of you.'"

How to Celebrate Lent?

One time, at least, we want to describe in greater detail how the celebrations in our institutions often come about. To celebrate the beginning of Lent, for example, we use the seasons of the year and our residents' world of experience.

Around Ash Wednesday life starts anew. Just one sunny spring day and our people revive. Singing, they go to school: The coming of springtime can actually be heard!

Here and there early flowers appear. The garden has systematically been prepared for spring. The old leaves have been raked together and the bushes pruned. All of the residents have been watching this. Some were allowed to help in burning the prunings. And now they notice how green blades in the flower boxes hesitantly emerge above the soil. Trees and bushes are about to burst open. New life is brewing in the air.

Spring is also a time in which people may become restless, as plants are repotted, seed boxes prepared. This is also a time to think of a "spring cleaning." All in all, an excellent period to dwell upon the "trash" within us, to do some thinking about all those dead things and matters that have somehow gotten stuck. Do we have courage enough to face up to that "trash" and clean it up so that the way will be cleared to a new life within ourselves and with each other? In a season in which so much sowing is going on, it's a good idea to dwell upon the question, Does the seed, as far as we are concerned, fall on rich soil? What kind of fruit do we actually produce?

From a Conversation on Ash Wednesday

"People have to fast!" one of them says. "When you don't eat and don't eat sweets so much, you become light." And saying this he slaps his fat tummy. "And when you are light, you go up to heaven much easier!"

"Ashes on your head make you grow!" someone else says. He had watched the gardener scattering ashes over the lawn. Those ashes were left over, after all the dead wood of pruned and blown off branches were burned.

"During Lent, Paul has to share his cigars with others. Jesus and Moniek [his group leader], have ordered him to do so."

Ben sees in the coming Lenten season a promising perspective. For during Lent, others have to share!

Preparation

As we reflect on the seasons of the year and on everything they call forth in our minds, the biblical stories emerge automatically. Would not the situation have been the same when Jesus told his stories for the first time? Would he not have followed the seasons? In the sowing time, he may have talked about the seed and the sower and about the unfruitful tree that needed new soil. But in the harvest time, he would have pointed out how people can be recognized by their fruit. There are people such as the Pharisees and the rich young man who hear the word of God but don't yield a harvest, while in the case of others, for instance, the Good Samaritan, the yield is large.

Of course, a choice has to be made, and finally we opt for the story of the Good Samaritan. It is extremely well suited to prepare our people for Lent. What's more, this story can be staged. And why shouldn't we shape all these beautiful thoughts into very tangible forms? We are going to burn trash to get ashes from which new life can arise again. We are going to try to save an almost dying big plant by pruning it and giving it fresh soil. Due to their own Catholic background (family or institutions) our people still have their own ideas about Lent. They have memories of the ashes, the purple vestments, the Lenten sweet tin for putting away the candies, the bread without jam. These recollections will play a part in the celebration of the First Sunday of Lent, and it will be a celebration close to their own world of experience.

The beginning of Lent will be celebrated in two parts, the first on Saturday afternoon and the second on Sunday morning. In the religious instructions preceding the celebrations, the following work scheme is used:

1. *A story.* A story is told to explain what fasting is all about. After all, this Good Samaritan has to abandon his donkey and all his belongings. First he has to free his hands in order to help this man along the road. Next, he gives him some of his own drinking water and pays the innkeeper out of his own money so that he can take good care of the injured victim. Everyone agrees: "What this Good Samaritan did could really be called fasting!" Only one of them takes a different view: "They should have called an ambulance!"

2. *A game.* After telling the story, it is staged. Paul plays the part of the Good Samaritan. Hearing the victim's cry for help, he comes to the rescue. But then he gets stuck. In order to help him he has to untie and put down a big cigar box tied to his hand with a piece of string. Wavering a lot whether to help or not, he finally puts the box down. Thus, with his two hands he is able to help the victim back onto his feet. But even in this situation he is just not able to give him a cigar.

By way of thanks, Paul gets a kiss. It is quiet for a moment. Are the others surprised? They don't know Paul as a man eager to help. But his gesture has gotten across. By renouncing your ties and thus freeing your hands, you are able to use them for others. That's fasting in a very concrete manner.

3. *A discussion.* In the discussion following the play, we elaborate on a few topics. We pay attention to the fact that things we are very attached to (like Paul to his cigar box) may become troublesome. Jos looks at his inevitable table knick-

knack and remains silent. Ed, with brown-stained fingers from smoking, remarks, "I am attached to a roll-up!" Thus, everyone thinks of something special, something hard to give up during Lent. Because fasting means keeping your hands free to be able to help others, opening your ears to be able to listen to someone else, clearing your mouth to be able to say something nice. Lent means making room for a new beginning.

4. *A plan.* We agree that all of us will search for things that are troubling us. The leaders of the various sections are informed of this proposition. A kind of spring cleaning gets under way.

The First Sunday in Lent

Saturday Afternoon: Clearing Away the Trash

We meet in the chapel, light a candle, and pray. A big copper vessel stands in the center. Later on the ashes will be put into it, but at this moment it is still empty. Everybody has brought along some trash. The pastor asks: "What shall we do with all this trash?" Someone suggests taking it to the refuse container in the back of the woods. "Ashes make the grass grow and the garden beautiful," a "gardener" tells the pastor.

The pastor explains: "God knows what to do with our human trash. Using it, he wants to make us new. Through it, he wants to help us grow so that we may become his good helpers." Doing evil or being troubled by someone else's evil ways could be called human "trash." On this topic they tackle each other in a lively manner: Paul, who is always attached to his cigars; others, with other attachments. On a black paper everyone writes down his own misdeeds, the things that have been bothering him and that he wants to clear away.

We are going to burn the trash, not in the woods but in the garden behind the chapel. We collect it, pile it up, and set it on fire. When the heap is burning nicely, everyone throws his black paper into the fire. That's what Ed does with his tobacco pouch. It was almost empty though!

Standing around the fire, we pray to God for forgiveness and ask him that we may become his good helpers for each other and for everyone who needs us. We pray to God to stay close to us, like the warmth of the fire and the light of the flames, and that he will make us new and beautiful. Then we sprinkle the flames with holy water. We have to be patient; it takes some time before we are able to collect the ashes. But once the fire has gone out, we shovel the warm ashes into the copper vessel. It makes quite a heap—more than enough to scatter over the heads so that something new will be able to grow. Solemnly, the vessel is carried into the chapel. We conclude the ceremony by changing the white altar linen for a purple one.

After praying the Our Father, we go home.

Sunday Morning: The Good Samaritan

At the beginning of the celebration we carefully light the candles in the still-dusky chapel. The more candles we light, the brighter everything becomes. We still must wait for the big light of Easter, the light that the Easter candle brings. First, lots of trash has to be cleared away.

After the lighting of candles, everyone's attention is fixed on the copper vessel filled with the ashes collected the evening before. Using three slides from the series *What the Bible Tells Us* (Utrecht: Docete), the pastor calls to mind once more how people hurt each other, how they make a real mess for each other, even abuse the earth: slide 1, a little girl in the midst of a devastated landscape; slide 2, quarreling students; slide 3, the Good Samaritan.

Next, the ashes in the copper vessel are blessed. Those who, like the Good Samaritan, want to roll up their sleeves, may now come forward. Those who want to empty their hands and give God a helping hand in making people and the land new and beautiful may now receive the ashes. And while the ashes are scattered over the residents' heads, we pray God, who created everything out of ashes and sand, to renew us by using the ashes of this trash.

What is left over is put into small pots in which hyacinths have been planted. Every resident receives a little pot to take home. Out of the dead ashes of the trash a beautiful, sweet-smelling flower will grow. While decay and death are still around, we hold in our hands a symbol of Easter, of the resurrection, a symbol of a new person. On Easter morning, the Easter candle will be surrounded by the same hyacinths, which by then will be flowering. We conclude the celebration with a prayer in which we ask for God's blessing.

Lent has started.

A Sunday in Lent:
The Barren Fig Tree

On one of the next few Sundays of Lent a big ficus, more than six feet high, is put into the chapel. It's a drooping plant: many branches don't have any leaves, and the ones still attached aren't very healthy at all. We all look at it. Remarks are made such as, "Probably it didn't get any water," and with disapproval, the dry soil is checked. "Probably it didn't get any light."

Then a discussion follows, and the question is raised whether it is still worthwhile to give this plant a chance. Most of the residents are in favor of throwing it onto the garbage dump or else on the other prunings so that it can be burned with them.

The pastor says that he will read a story from the Book of God. In his own words he tells the story of the barren fig tree (Luke 13:6-9), a story in which Jesus talks about a tree that looked bad. "That tree," the pastor explains, "couldn't bear fruit. The soil was exhausted and not fertile any more. It lacked plant fertilizer." The story doesn't sound unfamiliar to our people. One resident, a farmer's son, explains that his father is using compost. Someone else shouts, "We could give this plant some new soil, too, couldn't we?"

That's what we are going to do. Once the ficus is out of the pot we notice how stale the soil smells. Someone opens a sack of potting soil. That smells much fresher! The old soil is shaken off into a wheelbarrow, and using their hands, two or three boys throw the rich soil into the pot, covering the roots on all sides. Someone thinks of asking the sacristan for holy water. While they are about it, they want to make a good job of it.

Next, the branches are examined. Someone who knows gives advice. He points out which branches have to be cut out, and where exactly, so new shoots can bud again.

In about twelve minutes the whole job is finished. We put the ficus where it can be seen by everyone. The pastor points out that Jesus needed the fig tree in order to explain something. "A narrative tree then!" someone exclaims. "Yes, a tree to explain something. A tree or plant may not perform well sometimes, and that happens with people, too. They may make things hard for each other. And then the reaction could be, As far as I'm concerned, you can drop dead! And in that case, as with the plant, you throw him away and won't give him another chance.

"With his story about that barren tree, Jesus wants to explain that God never pushes people out, not even the annoying ones. He always gives people a new chance. And that's the way Jesus acts. He always tries to see the good in everyone. As long as there is some good—and that holds for every human being—a person may be fully cured again."

In a prayer we thank God for his love of us. We thank him, too, for giving us a new chance, for his willingness to never give up on us. We ask him that we may become new so that we won't write off or push out other people.

Next we celebrate Holy Mass.

After we finish the celebration, we choose a good new spot for our plant. We decide to put it in the hall of the school. Everyone is invited to keep an eye on it. And thanks to all the good care, the ficus makes it. Later on, we proudly gather around it. It was a good idea, after all, to give this plant another chance. Everyone agrees.

Palm Sunday:
Hosanna for the New King

Preparation

On Palm Sunday, Holy Week begins. Easter is already in sight, but before that, there is a long way yet to go. Jesus still has to go his way of the cross. We are going to commemorate this on Holy Thursday and Good Friday.

There is a shadow cast over this day. After all, Jesus enters Jerusalem to take up his cross and die. Yet there is something to celebrate, and Jesus is cheered on loudly as a good king who knows what people need, who loves them and throws himself into the breach for them. With his own life, he will guarantee their well being. He is a king after God's heart, and he brings God's kingdom to the people. Risen on the third day, he himself will be the first one to participate in that kingdom. On Palm Sunday, we are allowed to get a little foretaste of it.

When such a king makes his festive entry into Jerusalem, he is rightly cheered on. That happened in Jerusalem at that time, and that is going to happen today, with streamers, flags, and music, and with all the candy sticking on the *palmpaases*, * first in the chapel and thereafter in the whole institution.

At the Palm Sunday celebration we make use of the following elements: the story of the entry, palm branches, a statue

---

Palmpaases, carried in Palm Sunday processions, are gaily decorated sticks to which small candies or other sweets have been attached.

of Jesus, flags and streamers, the *palmpaases,* and a brass band.
The preparation is done as follows:

• In a number of catechetical sections, the story about Jesus'
entry is told, discussed, and worked out.

• To decorate the chapel, flags and streamers are made.

• Under the guidance of the creative therapist, a statue of
Jesus is made by two residents. Solemnly, it will be carried
into the chapel and will be carried in procession around the
home.

• At a number of living quarters, *palmpaases* are decorated.
In a small pamphlet intended for the leaders, the pastor has
written down a few lines on the meaning and the use of
these *palmpaases.* This will enable the leaders to give some
explanations while the group is working on them.

• On the Saturday before Palm Sunday, the pastor takes
some of the boys with him into the woods to cut off palm
branches. He seizes the opportunity to explain to them
what's so special about such small palm branches.

The entire preparation has been organized and performed
by the pastor and two volunteers in cooperation with a number of group leaders.

The Liturgy

The chapel is filling up. Flags, streamers, and *palmpaases* are
brought along. It is being decorated, and everyone helps out.
When all are seated and it is quiet again, a slide from the series
What the Bible Tells Us is shown. We see Jesus entering the city
accompanied by people waving palm branches and making
music on flutes and tambourines. Using the slide, the pastor
explains briefly the feast we are celebrating today. Next, we
sing together a song about the entry into Jerusalem, composed
by one of the group leaders.

The Solemn Entry

The statue is carried into the chapel by the two residents who have been taking care of it. The result of their efforts is very striking and beautiful: Jesus dressed in a red robe. It is something for them to be proud of, and they get the appreciation they deserve—enthusiastic applause. Then the statue is placed on the colorfully decorated altar, and the pastor tells the residents how Jesus entered Jerusalem and how enthused the people were.

After this story, one of the residents plays the organ. Some of them have brought along their recorders, triangles, or tambourines. They gather around Jesus' statue and make music. The others join in, clapping their hands.

A girl steps forward and puts her *palmpaas* on the altar table. To her sorrow, a boy who has brought nothing along picks a few sweets off her stick. He waves his hands, showing how delicious they are. Taking up this small incident, the pastor asks everyone to let the one next to him taste the *palmpaas*. That's done. Tasting and eating the sweets, they are engaged with each other for a moment.

We thank God for such a good king who brings heaven down onto earth for a moment, right here, close to us.

The Blessing of the Palms

The basket with palm branches is brought into the chapel. They are distributed, one to everyone present. Then each person steps forward and first bows before the statue, then fastens a palm branch to the procession cross. Meanwhile, we sing a hymn to the great king, repeating it several times.

The last branch is attached to the procession cross, which stands behind the statue and rises above it. Once more the pastor points out the importance of such a little palm. While the branches of the other trees look dead at this time of year, the small leaves of the palm branches are green. Such a green branch applies well to Jesus and the feast of his entry as the new king. With the palms in our hands we think of Easter, even though Jesus still has to suffer and die.

The pastor also explains how to use the palm branches: "Take it home after the service and hang it on the wall so you won't forget what happened on Palm Sunday and Easter. And when someone is ill or grieved, take your palm and bless that person and pray: 'Jesus, good king, take care of . . . who suffers or is grieved. Amen.' " And of course we practice this together. Next, the pastor blesses the palm branches with holy water, and the palm song is sung.

The Palm Procession

Then the palm procession starts. The pastor lifts the statue of Jesus from the altar. He invites everyone to go outside, walking behind the statue. After all, Jesus is not only a good king here in the chapel, but in the whole institution, and for all the people who live and work here.

Meanwhile, a brass band is lined up in front of the chapel. Led by the music, we move through the building. It's a colorful procession with its *palmpaases* and flags. Finally the procession arrives at the chapel garden, where the statue is placed upon a decorated platform. For a few minutes we pray together, and after singing the palm song once more, everyone goes home.

A few days later, a group leader tells me that after the celebration two residents brought a palm branch to the ward. They explained what it was used for and gave a demonstration of how it could be used when somebody was ill.

Holy Thursday:
Out of Sight but Not Out of Mind

Preparation

In the celebration of Holy Thursday we commemorate together the Last Supper. At that meal Jesus met with his disciples for the last time, and he bade farewell to them. To say good-bye fits well into the residents' world of experience within the institution. What good-bye means, they experience every time a loved group leader or another acquaintance leaves for good. Out of sight is then very often out of mind, too; that's the way it is. Yet there are some who left whose memory will never fade. Stories about them are still going around. Some of the residents still have a picture or keep a knickknack they received from them. These friends are not with us any longer, but they live on in stories and memories.

We begin with this concrete experience of life as we build the catechesis for the Last Supper. Jesus, too, says good-bye, and he, too, leaves behind a living, life-giving memory: bread to break, wine to drink. And then there is the story about the washing of the feet as a last act of charity toward his friends, a last gesture of concern about their total well being. Bread, wine, washing of feet. Signs that still make him present, although he isn't here any more. We will celebrate this presence under the motto "Out of Sight but Not Out of Mind!"

The catechesis to prepare for this celebration takes place on Wednesday afternoon and Thursday morning in Holy Week. The liturgy centers around the washing of the feet and the bread and the cup. By way of introduction, a slide from the series *What the Bible Tells Us* is used for each part: Jesus washing his apostles' feet, and Jesus distributing bread and wine.

In the afternoon, preceding the celebration, we, together with a few residents, get the chapel ready. The flower decorations are brought in, and the basin gets its proper place. Jesus' statue is placed on the altar again. Instead of the red robe, which goes with Palm Sunday, a white one is now draped around it. The little cups are filled with wine, and the matzos are put on a big, beautiful plate. All these items we bought, together with the residents, in a store. Finally, the chairs are arranged in a circle around the altar.

The Liturgy

By seven o'clock the residents enter the chapel. All are visibly surprised by the decorations. Some of them have brought along souvenirs of parents or friends they have had to take leave of. When everyone is seated, the pastor welcomes the group on the occasion of this special evening. After all, it's the evening of the Last Supper, the evening on which Jesus bade his friends farewell. But it isn't that far yet. This evening we still can sing, "Friends sing in joy, for the Lord is here" (*Randstad Collection*, no. 71).

To Say Good-bye

For many of our people, the words "farewell," "goodbye," evoke mixed feelings. Spontaneously they mention the names of group leaders who left us, recently or a long time ago. Sometimes a touch of bitterness can be heard in their voices. Pete is honest about that: "They are no good use to us. Once you are used to them, they leave again." But there are others who point out that there are new ones who came to replace them. And that we are happy with them, too.

Thea tells about Mimi. She shows a little doll Mimi gave her when she left. And Pete takes out his tobacco pouch, a keepsake from his father. Two memories simultaneously evoke nostalgia and solidarity, renewing the pain of farewell, yet somehow consoling and bonding those left behind.

Just like Mimi and Pete's father, Jesus did not want to leave without leaving behind a memorial. In this way, even after he had gone, his friends could remain united with him and with each other. And so Jesus left behind bread to break and wine to drink as a sign that he would stay with them even after he had left. But that's not all. He did something else. Listen!

The Washing of the Feet

The pastor tells the story: "Before Jesus had dinner, he washed his friends' feet. Peter felt that this was ridiculous. He did not want Jesus to go down on his knees for him, humiliating himself by washing his feet. But Jesus said to Peter and the others: 'Only in this way can I show you that I am your helper and not your boss. Only in this manner can I show you that I love all of you from head to foot. And you, do the same. That's what God our Father wants us to do.'"

Next the pastor fills the basin. He asks who wants to wash the feet of the others, just like Jesus did. Hein stands up and says, "Feet stink!" He wouldn't touch it! And he gains support: "Yes, feet stink!" It turns out to be difficult, the pastor continues, to love someone from top to toe, to love someone's good points but also those that are disagreeable. To go down on one's knees for someone else, to show an interest in all that's base, to start with somebody, literally, from scratch, isn't as easy as one thinks. To get along with people that way is quite an art, and Jesus was a master at it.

Hein steps forward. His shoelaces are loose, and he isn't able to tie them himself. He asks the pastor whether he would be so kind as to help him. The pastor is willing to help, but he keeps standing upright. And obviously, he can't reach Hein's laces. Someone shouts that the pastor has to go on his knees if he really wants to help. And indeed, this way he succeeds. Hein is glad. Still sitting on his knees, the pastor explains what has actually happened.

The example turns out to be effective. Koos has taken off his shoes and socks. Hermien is going to wash his feet. Hein watches but keeps silent. Still others start washing each other's feet. The pastor dries them while he calls everyone by name: "Clara, Jan, Teun, you are lovable from top to toe. Act just like Jesus, then everybody will become happy. Amen!"

With a mixture of restraint and glee, Hein asks whether he may wash the pastor's feet. He doesn't object. Hein goes down on his knees for himself and for someone else. There is laughter. Nobody had expected Hein to do this.

We conclude the washing of the feet with a prayer.

Bread and Wine

The pastor stands behind the altar table next to Jesus' statue—the same one that was carried in the Palm Sunday procession. He invites everyone to come and sit down around him. They all pull up their chairs or wheelchairs.

The slide of the Last Supper is being projected. This calls for associations. They point to what they recognize, even Judas. We sing "My God What a Joy" (*Randstad Collection,* no. 74). Then the pastor says, "Now we are going to do what Jesus did. He took the bread, broke it into pieces, and said to his friends: 'This bread, it is I. It has been broken into pieces so that it can be distributed to every one of you. Eat it, so that we remain united.' " The pastor breaks the matzos into pieces and hands them out. When Thea receives hers, she says: "Now I have two of them. This one," and she points to the little doll, "is from Mimi, and that one" the piece of matzo, "is from Jesus."

Then the pastor says, "Jesus also took a cup of wine. 'This wine, it is I,' he said. 'It is for you. Drink of it.' " He gives everyone a little cup with some wine and repeats Jesus' words to his disciples: "When I am gone after a while, you should do the same as I am doing now. Thus, I am with you, and you won't be left empty-handed, and this will comfort all of you. In this way, we will remain united until I return."

Joining hands, we sing a hymn together. We have formed a strong circle with Jesus in our midst. Still holding hands, we say the intercessory prayers, and we conclude the service by praying an Our Father and singing a hymn of thanksgiving.

Now the hour of farewell has come. Jesus goes to the Mount of Olives, a garden close by. He is terrified by what is going to happen, for he knows, all too well, that Judas has betrayed him. He asks his friends to stay with him while he asks his Father to help him. But they fall asleep. They find it difficult to say good-bye.

Quietly Hein carries Jesus' statue out of the chapel. Everyone goes home now. But first everybody gets a matzo to break and share with those residents who weren't able to come today.

Good Friday:
On Guard at the Cross

Preparation

At the celebration of Good Friday we commemorate Jesus' suffering and death. Pain, grief, death, and the feeling of being let down are experiences a number of our people are quite familiar with. For many of them, such experiences have been very personal. And so, in our liturgical celebration there should be room for these personal stories and experiences. Only in this way will our residents be able to experience on Easter morning the feeling of joy that the resurrection brings.

This day's liturgy will consist of two parts. First, we will meditate and dwell upon our Lord's suffering and death. To help us, we will use a set of four slides from the series *What the Bible Tells Us:* slide 1, Jesus before Pilate; slide 2, Jesus carrying his cross; slide 3, Jesus meeting Veronica; slide 4, Jesus hanging on the cross, with Mary and John next to him, under the cross.

In the second part, a veneration of the cross will be held. For that purpose, a large wooden cross has been erected in the chapel. Those who attend will get the opportunity to decorate it with flowers and also with all the items they'll bring along as a memory of their own grief or that of their acquaintances.

It is obvious that the liturgy of Good Friday requires careful catechetical preparation. Time for this is set aside in the morning, before the afternoon celebration. Since on that day quite a few residents are going home, the number of participants in the liturgy itself will be rather small.

The decoration of the chapel has been kept austere. A purple cloth covers the altar table. On it are four candles. In front of the altar, our large wooden cross has been erected.

The Liturgy

As the parishioners enter the chapel, music of the *Mattheus Passion* can be heard. Some of the residents have brought along something that reminds them of their own grief or that of others: pictures of friends or family who have passed away, a newspaper picture of a war scene, Pete's tobacco pouch that was his father's. There are also some residents who have brought along their own little crucifix.

Meditative Narration of the Passion

After a short greeting, we make the sign of the cross and pray together. Next, Peter, one of the residents, plays on the organ "O Head Full of Blood and Wounds." Then Jan, Clara, and Hein step forward and stand next to the pastor. They were the ones who helped in preparing this service. Jan holds in his hands the crown of thorns. He made it with the help of one of the gardeners. Clara carries Veronica's cloth on which is a picture of Jesus with the crown of thorns. Assisted by the creative therapist, Clara made it herself. Hein's task will be to stand guard at the cross. All three of them have prepared their own little prayer.

Using the four slides, the pastor tells about Jesus' passion and death. Afer the first narration there is a moment's silence. Then Peter plays the organ again, and Jan solemnly hangs the crown of thorns on the cross and says his prayer. This unpretentious ritual recurs after every slide. Clara attaches her cloth to the cross and prays. After the third slide, it's Hein's turn to say his prayer. The Gregorian *Stabat mater* is played on the organ as soon as the fourth passion scene has been shown. Now it is the pastor's turn to lead in prayer.

The meditative part of the celebration is concluded by singing a song about the cross.

Veneration of the Cross

First the cross is put in the center of the chapel. The pastor points out that the cross was standing on a mountain so that everyone could clearly see how Jesus spread out his arms for all people. After all, he loves everybody, and God acts the same way. Jesus will do anything for us. Thus he became our Redeemer, the help and support of everyone who is grieved or who suffers. Jesus' cross tells us over and over again: I love every one of you, and that is from head to toe. The pastor asks all who are present to cross themselves with that painful sign of love, avowing: "God loves us, God loves everyone from head to toe, the Father, the Son, and the Holy Spirit."

Meanwhile, Jan and Clara, their arms filled with tulips, move next to the cross. Everybody may now step forward to venerate the cross and to pray for whatever intentions he or she may have.

Bert prays for his father, who recently passed away. He shows pictures and lays them down near the cross. He becomes distressed, but Hein grabs hold of him. That is his prayer for Bert. Nico prays for the war in the Persian Gulf and pins a newspaper photo to the cross.

Agaath brings along her heavily battered doll. She tells about it. The pastor asks her to put her doll near the cross. Instead, she takes a flower and comes and stands up under the cross herself.

Peter shows his father's tobacco pouch but immediately puts it in his pocket again. With a thumbtack he pins a flower to the cross. This is his memory of and his prayer for his father.

Thijs has his recorder with him. He plays on it. That's his way of praying. Many others follow. They all pin a flower to the cross, talk about the grief they know, or mention the names of members of their families or acquaintances they love. Thus the cross gradually tells about everyone's grief and affection, becoming a symbol of life's joys and sorrows, of God and his people.

Life's sweet and bitter is expressed once more in the intercessory prayers. After every one of them Hein lights a candle, and after the last one is lit we pray that it soon may become Easter. Clara puts the last of the flowers at the foot of the cross.

Together we pray the Our Father, and while Peter plays the organ, everyone quietly leaves.

Low Sunday:
The Men of Emmaus

It is the Sunday after Easter. Today the theme of the celebration will be the men of Emmaus. But first, because many residents went home at Easter, they spend some time catching up with each other.

The Liturgy

After the opening prayer, while showing two slides, the pastor tells the story of the men of Emmaus. Both were living in Emmaus at that time and were disciples of Jesus. After Jesus' death they returned home because Jesus had not done what he had promised. Life had not become heaven on earth.

Thijs, the Man of Emmaus

The pastor asks if there is anybody in the chapel who resembles one of those men of Emmaus. Thijs reacts: "They promise a lot, but to keep their words . . . " What happened? Thijs' brother is traveling a lot. During the days after Easter he was to have come on a visit, but as he had to leave sooner, he sent a postcard instead. "A postcard, what's the use of that?" Thijs lowers his head. The pastor draws him closer and puts him on a little stool, all by himself. Because that's the way Thijs feels right now. Trudy is Thijs' chum. She comes up to him but Thijs doesn't—or does not want to—see her.

The pastor points out that the men of Emmaus talked and acted about the same way as Thijs is acting now. They, too, lowered their heads and said: "Jesus had promised so, but then . . . too bad . . . let's go home." It was entirely clear, they had had enough of it. But on the way home, someone came and walked along with them. And just like Trudy, who is with Thijs now, the stranger listened to them carefully, and he talked with them. And then, when they came home and went to the table, they recognized him. This stranger was Jesus, because he broke the bread for them. So Jesus was still with them, but completely different from what they had imagined. And they ran back to town to tell the apostles what had happened.

And Thijs? What kind of gesture is he now in need of, to feel a little confident again? Reaching out to Thijs, Trudy grabs his arms. Thijs gets back on his feet, and she leads him along. Thijs says that the postcard is hanging in his room. "So your brother did not forget you, did he?" the pastor says. "After all, he is concerned about you, but different from what you had imagined. He showed his concern with a postcard!"

An Unexpected Event

Meanwhile, Frans enters the chapel. As usual, he is late. He walks straight to the altar and stands next to it holding a mourning card in his hand. As soon as he sees an opportunity to chime in, he has his say: "Opa died!"

The pastor asks him to have patience for a moment so as to be able to finish Thijs and Trudy's story first. But that takes too long for Frans. He grabs the pastor's vestment and drags him toward the Easter candle. Next, he puts the mourning card against it. Then he takes the pastor's hands, folds them, and says: "Pray!" (Frans had participated intensively in the Holy Week and Easter Vigil celebrations.)

Then Lex stands up. He has difficulty speaking and moves about clumsily. He cries: "Papa," pointing to himself. Last year he lost his dad. The pastor asks him to come forward and to explain what he wants. With a lot of fussing and stumbling over his legs, he leaves his place, puts his arms around Frans' shoulders, and pointing first to Frans and then to himself, repeats again: "Papa, dead!" Frans corrects: "Opa," but Lex doesn't care. Drawing Frans with him, he clears a chair in the first row and sits down. Then he takes Frans on his knees and wraps his arms around him in a kind of Pietà tableau. That's Lex's way of expressing his pity for, and solidarity with, Frans.

Ruud, who is an altar boy this morning, gets to his feet, takes a candle from the altar, and puts it in front of Lex, still holding Frans on his lap. He does this in a grave yet humorous manner. Gradually the buzzing quiets down. Fascinated and smiling, everybody looks on. Frans frees himself from Lex, takes the mourning card from the Easter candle, and returns to his chair. Applause follows. Thijs says, "Lex acts like Jesus. Trudy and I, too!" He shakes hands with Frans. Quite a few come forward and do the same. This clearly does Frans a lot of good.

As soon as peace has been restored, we sing a song in honor of Jesus' name.

The bowl with hosts and the cup with wine are put on the altar. Above hangs a picture of Jesus breaking bread amidst the men of Emmaus. In the Communion prayer the pastor says that every time we break bread and drink wine together, Jesus—in his own person— is with us. He helps us make the right gesture toward each other, the way Trudy and Lex and all the others did when they shook hands with Frans. At the blessing, Lex stands next to the pastor and gives the benediction along with him. He tells Frans that he is going to have coffee with him later.

Monday morning, a leader of Frans' section calls. She wants to know what happened in the chapel on Sunday. Frans had been full of it all day long but didn't have words to tell about it.

How to Celebrate the Healing Stories?

What is the best way to read and celebrate the healing stories of the Gospel with our patients? After all, we are well aware that our patients could never experience miraculous healings like those described in the Gospel. This is a question that has kept us busy for a long time. Besides, the answer to that question has everything to do with the very core and meaning of our work.

A description of three celebrations will be presented here. Each of them centers around a healing story. The most appropriate time to conduct these services would be the Easter season. After all, healing stories are actually nothing but stories about the resurrection. We include our own reflections on these healing stories, as they relate to mentally disabled persons.

The residents of our institutions are mentally handicapped. Many of them not only suffer from a mental disability but from physical disabilities, as well. Some of them can hardly walk. To "come along" they have to depend on a cane, a walker, or a wheelchair. Others are deaf, or at least hard of hearing. Some find it hard to express themselves or cannot speak at all. Some grope around in half-light because they are blind or partially sighted. Then there are those who, prisoners of their own rage, know all too well what it means to be forced to live outside the group.

The healing stories in the Gospel always dealt with and are still dealing with people like these. Jesus meets them, suffering and in distress, and he heals them. He understands their vigorous protests and confirms their longing for wholeness. Being physically or mentally disadvantaged is neither God's will nor his punishment. Jesus is on their side, and he shows it. In this respect he differs from those people who would silence handicapped people trying to voice their grievances about their miserable condition. Unlike others, Jesus never tries to persuade them to resign to their fate. To resign to and to accept one's condition are quite different propositions. By healing those disabled people, Jesus gave them a future. And not only them but all others who would come after them. For them, his cures become signs of the kingdom, incentives not to despair.

But also for us, bystanders, the healing stories contain many lessons. As we follow Jesus' example, they encourage us to show our solidarity with these disabled and handicapped people. Their pain must never be evaded. We must always beware that our residents, as persons, are never reduced to their handicap or ailment, never resigned to the tyranny of their destiny.

But of course we should always be realistic. After all, it was Jesus who made the lame walk and the deaf hear. We cannot perform miracles. Our residents are well aware of that. But still, they let us know sometimes how they long to be healed. A wheelchair is nothing but a makeshift, a substitute. The pain caused by this unfulfilled desire should never be obscured or talked down. Consequently, we have to be careful not to present Christ in our stories as a kind of magician. A much better approach would be to help our residents recognize how some of Jesus' healing power for the sick of his day is still working, right now, in the care and help given them by therapists and group leaders. With this perspective, there is cause to celebrate small miracles. This way, helpers and residents alike get the opportunity to present to God all that is on their minds: the struggle to keep up the fight, the moments of discouragement and failure.

The liturgy is where this may happen. With Jesus' stories in our hands, we help each other to carry on. The healing stories offer a glimpse of the kingdom. They are an inspiration for all of us to become more and more imaginative and creative in our dealings with disadvantaged people. These stories are an impelling force never to cease in our efforts to assist them in their plight. The point is that every effort should be made to preserve, and if need be, to restore, our residents' dignity as sons and daughters of God and fellow human beings.

Keeping this in mind, we celebrate these services. And not just the pastor and assistants. In our institutions many people function as physiotherapists, speech therapists, physicians, psychologists, group leaders. Tenaciously and with lots of ingenuity, they are constantly helping these disabled people, created as they are in God's image and likeness, to preserve or restore their dignity. When asked to help prepare these liturgical services, most of them are immediately willing to help. In this way the biblical healing stories become actualized in the lives of mentally and physically handicapped people. Together we celebrate our residents' revolt and our solidarity, presenting to God each other's grief and joy.

The Cure of the Man
Who Was Paralyzed

Preparation

Among the residents of our institutions there are many who can hardly walk, others who can't walk at all. Every day, they have to cope again with the burden of their disability. Sometimes they revolt against their plight and ask why Jesus does not perform miracles anymore, why he does not make them walk again.

The physiotherapists, who do their utmost to assist these people, are the first to whom the pastor presents his plans. In cooperation with residents who are crippled or condemned to wheelchairs, he wants to reenact the Gospel story about the cure of a paralytic. Without any hesitation, all the specialists pledge their full support. This agreement is followed by sessions in which each one gives an extensive account of the treatment used and the feelings experienced while treating their patients.

Subsequently the pastor meets with those residents who are willing to play a part in the liturgy service. When asked whether they would be willing to hand over their orthopedic aids to be used as a part of the liturgy, none of them raised any objections. And thus it happens that at the beginning of the service, braces, cases, orthopedic shoes, a plaster bed, and a cane are lying on the altar table or resting against it. During the celebration we make use of some slides from the series *What the Bible Tells Us,* this time about the cure of the paralytic.

The Liturgy

After the residents enter the chapel and find the inner peace to look around, they discover immediately what this service is all about. One of them says, "John can't walk either!" And Alex, with braces himself, says, "I have got the same ones!" He uses a walking frame and asks whether his walker is needed, too. The pastor kindly accepts it and invites Alex to join the others around the altar. Gerrit, Willem, and René, all using wheelchairs, also want to have a little spot near the altar table. Daan comes and offers his cane. When two physiotherapists enter the chapel, they are warmly greeted by all their patients with "You are trying to help us walk, too!" We open the service with a prayer and song. Using some slides, the pastor tells the story of the cure of a paralytic, approximately as follows:

"There was a man who from his early youth could not walk. That was awful. But what he resented most was that he could never walk where he wanted to go. He was lucky though, for when he grew older he had friends. They liked him very much and wished him all the best. But no matter how much the poor man tried, he wasn't able to walk. So his good friends came up with a solution. Putting him on a sheet, they carried him along wherever they went. Thus the crippled man's life became brighter, and he felt a deep sense of gratitude toward his wonderful benefactors. But his friends weren't quite satisfied. They wanted for the paralytic the very best. That is the way friends are. Once they learned that Jesus was passing that way, and, still carrying their friend on a sheet, they went to see him. To one another they said, 'Jesus won't let us down. He never gives up on people.'

"When they arrived at the house where Jesus stayed, they saw that it was crowded with people. There was no way of getting through, let alone with their crippled friend between them. By way of the roof might be the only solution. And so the lame man was lowered by his friends through an opening in the roof, right in front of Jesus' feet. They told him their story. Jesus saw how much they loved this crippled man. He decided to help the best way he could. Taking the paralytic's hand, he said: 'I heal you of your sins as well as of your ailment.' That is the way God is, and this story is the way I want to tell this to you. The paralytic got up and walked.''

It's quiet for a moment. Then René starts talking. He says he is glad he has a wheelchair and doesn't have to lie on a sheet. Willem reacts: ''If Jesus were only here, maybe I could walk again.'' These reactions fit in with the story. The pastor asks, ''Do you also have friends like that who listen to you and wish the best for you and perhaps even pray for you?'' Fortunately, they do have such friends. René points to Cor. Willem calls Jan, and others call out to their friends. The altar becomes crowded. We move the altar table to the center of the chapel so that there is room for everyone. Cor drives René around the table. The bystanders applaud. Cor is quite embarrassed. Grasping Cor's hand, René says, ''He doesn't let me down either!'' After the slide with the four men lowering the paralytic in front of Jesus' feet, the pastor shows one of Cor with René. The next one shows Janet, the physiotherapist, treating Willem, who then points at her. Janet explains how she helps keep Willem's legs flexible, and says that he can stand on his feet for a few moments. And she demonstrates this on the spot. And, really, Willem does stand on his feet for a few moments, but then he falls into her arms. He radiates joy with this small victory and earns a warm applause. The pastor explains that Janet likes Willem and therefore knows very well what he needs. She understands him, and Willem trusts her. And because of these mutual feelings, something in Willem's mind and body starts moving. Isn't that a small miracle?

Janet continues her story and explains how she, in turn, gets help from the shoemaker, who makes ''difficult shoes.'' The maker of orthopedic footwear working in his shop is shown on the next slide. Under the watchful eyes of Janet and the physician, the shoemaker is taking Erik's measurements for a pair of shoes. Janet shows how the support of the braces helps Alex and how a cast prevents Irma's arm from growing crooked.

Just like Jesus and those four men with their paralytic friend, there are still people who wish the best for someone else and never give up: Janet, the maker of orthopedic shoes, Cor and René, Willem and Alex. And because of this, small miracles still happen everyday. Willem is able to stand on his feet for a few moments. Because of his braces Alex no longer falls down. Who could have thought that? And this way heaven comes closer, little by little, day by day.

We start singing a hymn of thanksgiving.

To walk like the paralytic of the Gospel, to be able to walk without braces, walker, or cane—this remains a dream. The cripples and stumblers are well aware of that. The symbols of grief for this unfulfilled desire are lying around us. To them, Theo adds his walker. And amidst all these things the pastor places the paten with hosts and the chalice with wine. Pointing at the altar, René says, "God is present, too!" He asks whether he may help to distribute Communion later on. And while, after forming a circle, all worshipers shake hands with one another and the symbols of grief and thoughtful care are amongst us, we pray.

Everyone in the circle says his or her own intercessory prayer. Sometimes it is hardly understandable. A few verbalize their feelings about their disability—the burden of it, the grief. But a "thank you" meant for Janet (that she may not leave), and for the doctor, and the maker of orthopedic shoes, can also be heard. Janet in her turn says a prayer for the boys and girls she is working with.

We sing a song for strength and support. And after a short table prayer, we receive Holy Communion. Sitting in his wheelchair and pushed by Cor, René reverently distributes Holy Communion. Is his handicap for a moment sublimated?

The Cure of the Man Who Was Deaf and Mute

In dealing with deaf or deaf-mute residents, a great deal of patience is needed. Enfolding them in your heart and loving them, you want to communicate with them. And when you don't succeed, you can often see their anger in their faces. Sometimes our residents also become angry if, notwithstanding all mutual efforts, you still don't understand them. Fortunately, when they want to explain something at all costs, they prove to be quite tenacious and don't let you off the hook easily. Many helpers have an infinite amount of patience and take great pleasure in their search for new forms of communication. Hanneke, the speech therapist, is definitely one of these.

Preparation

As part of the preparation for the liturgy service, we pay Hanneke a brief visit and share with her all we have planned around these difficult healing stories. Highly enthusiastic, we talk about her work, and during this conversation the outline of the service crystallizes itself.

Jesus deals with a deaf-mute. He takes suffering to heart. Following his example, we want to be as caring for the deaf and the residents with speech impediments in our community as he was in his day. Perhaps we will be able to make others

52

experience what it means to be deaf and how awful it is not to be able to express oneself properly because of a speech defect. We call attention to the deaf and mute in our midst, and we want to show that one can also communicate with them, albeit in a different manner.

Hanneke, the speech therapist, is immediately prepared to help in the preparations for the service. She is also willing to play an active role in that celebration. After all, it is also her work and the small miracles performed by the communication department that are to be celebrated.

The Liturgy

Hanneke is present with the boys and girls of her department. Jeanette is one of them. Her bicycle is standing next to the altar. The letters HS (hard of hearing) are engraved on a red and white plate on the mudguard.

The pastor starts the service with a word of introduction. He reminds everyone of the previous Sundays, when we read the stories about the paralytic and the man who was confused. As it turns out, everyone remembers these stories very well. Today, the pastor continues, we read in the Book of God our Father of someone who was not able to hear. Meanwhile, he points to the plate on the bicycle. He is articulating well so that Jeanette is able to read his lips. She nods, indicating that she understands some of the story the pastor is talking about. He also tries to emphasize his words with gestures. And using her professional sign language, Hanneke translates whatever isn't being grasped by her patients. To start the service, all emphatically make the sign of the cross, and then we continue with the prayers. Whatever the pastor says or prays, Hanneke translates into sign language. This way, Jeanette is also able to join in prayer: "God our Father, we appreciate that you love us. When no one loves us, we feel ill at ease and grieved. Today, God our Father, we want just like Jesus to pay attention to all those people who have difficulty in hearing and talking. We want to sense how awful that is. Open our hearts, so that we don't let them down. Amen."

The pastor tells the story about the cure of the deaf-mute (Mark 7:31-37). He points out that here again there are good friends who don't let the deaf man down. That is the way good friends are. They carry him along until they find someone who is able to do something for him. Jesus appreciates the loving care of these friends, and he sympathizes with the deaf man. He cures him of his deafness. He has the power to do that.

Then, using sign language, Hanneke takes over: "Do you have any idea how awful it is not being able to hear? You see people move their lips and make gestures, but you don't hear a thing. You have to guess what others are talking about. This is the way Jeanette, too, has to see what I am talking about." Jeanette, fully endorsing this, nods, indicating she understands. "Do all of you want to experience this yourselves? Put your fingers into your ears and watch my lips very carefully. I am going to tell you a story by articulating every word very clearly, and you have to try to SEE what I am talking about."

They all plug their ears with their fingers. At first they laugh, but soon you could hear a pin drop. All eyes are fixed on Hanneke telling her story. And really, she is only moving her lips soundlessly while also making gestures. (That Hanneke's performance would be soundless, we had not told the residents beforehand.)

After a while many of them start wondering. Secretly they unplug their ears and start listening—but how come they don't hear anything? And yet they see Hanneke talking emphatically! Confusion ensues. First there are a few, but soon more and more of the residents don't plug their ears any longer. They look at each other in disbelief. Some of them even become a bit panicky, until Hanneke, much to their relief, speaks aloud again.

Then she explains what just happened. Obviously, some of them all of a sudden became scared of becoming deaf. Deaf people can also be scared and distrustful at times.

After that, Jeanette demonstrates with her deaf friends how they, using their hands, are able to communicate. Jeanette tells something in sign language. Her "pupils," still learning, try to guess what she is talking about.

Someone shows a "talk-script," a notebook with symbols. These signs enable a patient to communicate. This aid is particularly important whenever arms or hands cannot be moved adequately. Also "signal-cards" are shown. These are used when important matters have to be shared. We know now that if we don't want to let Jeanette down, we have to speak with her in a different manner. We decide, for this service, to use signal-cards for our prayer candle. Underneath the candle for the sick we hang a card with streamers and a little flag. Then the candles are lit. Jeanette lights one for all deaf people and for those who aren't able to talk.

As part of the intercessory prayer, Jeanette prays for her mother, who recently passed away and now stays with God our Father. All of us also pray for patience and that we may learn to talk with our hands. We also thank God for all those who help deaf people and for those with speech defects to be able to communicate. We are grateful for these small miracles of love. Before we prepare the altar, Jeanette is asked how one can show, using sign language, that one loves somebody. Stroking her cheek with the palm of her hand, she points to someone. That is the way she expresses love toward another person. Before Holy Communion at the liturgical sign of peace, we use sign language to show that we love one another. Hanneke, Jeanette, and her good friends stand around the altar table. After all, doesn't Jesus want them to be very close to him?

At the sign of peace, here and there a tear glistens.

Candles

A candle doesn't relieve from prayer
but is its continuation.
It is no substitute for a sacrifice
but it is its sign.
It does not obtain all
for which we pray
but it is a symbol of our trust.

(Text on the candle table at Huize Ursula)

The candle is a symbol of light. It has always played an important role in Christianity. The candle represents the light that shines in our darkness, but it is also a symbol of ourselves. Lighting a candle for someone else is not "shirking" one's responsibility. By lighting a candle you want to recommend someone else to the love of God. At the same time you want to be a shining light for that person. "The deepest meaning of life is, like a candle, to melt away in truth and love for God— to become light and glow" (R. Guardini, *Of Holy Symbols*, 46).

The Prayer Candle

Our people love candles. To light one for somebody is something important, an almost holy event. In every celebration, every time we say the intercessory prayers, in reverent silence candles are lit. Our prayer candle has seven candles. At the beginning of the celebration, four of them are already burning. They represent the set of intentions for which there can never be prayer enough: for the sick, those celebrating their birthdays, the dads and moms at home, and all those we cannot forget who are with God our Father. The last three candles are only lit when we have together decided what intentions we are going to pray for.

These three often turn out to be far too few.

The Cure of the Man Who Was Blind

Preparation

Mieke is blind. Moreover, she has cerebral palsy. She needs to be helped with everything. Yet she always looks cheerful. In all kinds of noise and tumult, she is able to recognize nearly everyone's voice. With a view to preparing for next Sunday's celebration, I first want to talk to Mieke. Anticipating this meeting, I feel some hesitancy. What kind of impression is the story of a man whose blindness was cured going to make on her? After all, Mieke has a reasonably good mind. The only reason she is a resident of our home is that she is so much in need of help.

I find her in the dayroom. I sit down next to her. The question uppermost in my mind is how she experiences her disability. Would not this Sunday be too painful for her?

I have just arrived in the dayroom when one of the leaders enters. He greets Mieke cordially. She in turn reminds him that she wants to come and see his new baby soon. Immediately, a date is fixed. "How are you going to look at the baby?" I ask her hesitantly. "That's very simple," Mieke says. "Simply hold, feel, and cuddle the baby." So, that's the way Mieke sees!

I wheel her outside. It's a lovely sunny day. In the wonderful park I sit down on a small bench next to her wheelchair. Together we listen to the birds and feel the sun. I tell her about Sunday and the story we are going to read, about the man who was blind but was cured. "Do you know what people in those days used to think of blindness?" I ask Mieke. "They thought of blindness as a punishment of God." At hearing that, Mieke laughs heartily. "Stupid, isn't it?" She reacts with self-assurance. Obviously, she doesn't feel like discussing this topic any further. Her blindness raises more questions in my mind than in hers. We chat for a while. I tell her that I am not only going to read the story but will also explain that it is stupid to think of God in that way. She thinks that would be a good idea.

During our conversation, the celebration begins to take a definite shape: We want to thank God for the gift of being able to see; we want to give personal attention to those who are blind or visually impaired; we want to explain to ourselves and to those attending the celebration in what manner we are able to help.

The Liturgy

That Sunday the weather is good. The celebration is held outside in the open air, on the beautiful field next to the chapel. Now the whole world, with the blue dome over it, is God's dwelling. Everybody thinks it's great and sits down comfortably in the grass. The pastor gives all a hearty welcome. He tells them that today we want to thank God our Father for all that we are able to see: "We are so used to this privilege that we take it for granted. But not everyone is blessed that way. Take, for instance, Mieke, sitting here next to me in her wheelchair. She isn't able to see all those beautiful colors!"

As an opening song, we sing "Look Around." After the song, we very consciously close our eyes for a moment. Then, very slowly, we open them again and look around, as if seeing things for the very first time. It's completely quiet. Everybody looks around. "Now look at each other and give a friendly nod to each other." We make a sign of the cross, and favored with the gift of vision, we pray: "Thanks, God our Father, for our eyes. Thanks for allowing us to see all the beauty that surrounds us. Help us to look at each other the proper way. We may need each other. Perhaps someone may need our eyes to see in her stead. Help us to use our eyes properly. Amen.''

Improvising, the pastor continues: ''Do you have any idea what it means to be blind? Touching with a white cane to try to find your way? Who of you wants to try it out?''

Two boys volunteer and are blindfolded. We put them outside the circle and have them find their way to the altar through all those who are sitting there. There is absolute silence as everyone watches. Along the way they get some assistance, but here and there they are teased. One of the boys is irritated and tries to sneak a look to see where he is. Once they arrive at the altar, they have to get rid of their anger about the teasing. Doing this to them while they couldn't see was really mean.

Next we read the story about Bartimaeus (Mark 10:46-52), and simultaneously, we have the story played out. One of the two boys who just finished his blindfold role is willing to continue the part a little longer and plays the role of the blind Bartimaeus. We put him on the floor with his begging-bowl in his hands. When the pastor tells how the blind man from the story calls for Jesus, our ''blind man,'' very audibly, does the same. He lives his role very well. When the man—at Jesus' word—is able to see again, our actor jumps up enthusiastically, makes a show-off kind of gesture, and earns warm applause.

With Mieke next to him, the pastor doesn't like to continue. Bartimaeus was cured—she isn't! ''Jesus was able to make people see. We aren't. But what we are definitely able to do is to help—or to tease. Just look what happened a few minutes ago!'' Mieke, too, is allowed to speak. She mentions all those who help her all the time. She is glad she is able to hear very well and is able to see ''with her hands.'' Together we get angry, for a moment, at all those dumb people who thought blindness a punishment of God. For a few moments we continue looking for ways that may enable us to bring some sunshine and light into Mieke's darkness and the darkness of others who are blind.

When we ask who of them wants to be such a helper, such a little sunshine, the answer is practically unanimous. Nearly everyone is willing to help. For everyone who volunteered, there is a badge to wear with a brilliant sun on it. We sing a song: "When you don't love each other." And during the celebration of the Mass, Mieke sits in her wheelchair next to the altar table.

After the celebration, about two hundred little suns go home. Weeks later, when they still walk around enthusiastically with their pinned-on suns, the sermon is still visible.

Pentecost:
He Breathed on Them

Preparation

For people who are only able to think in concrete terms, Pentecost remains a difficult feast. Just imagine! Jesus dies— but is still alive, even though that life is different from what it was before. On Ascension Day Jesus goes back to God his Father, but on Pentecost he returns through his Spirit. Who in the world is able to follow all that?

Yet Pentecost and the stories that surround it offer us some beautiful ideas: There is something that looks like fire, there is the wind blowing, and doors are thrown open. Then there is that strong liturgical gesture, the ceremony where the light of the Easter candle is put out. The light of the Easter candle can be extinguished, for it continues within the people who take it over and make it shine in the lives of others.

Our residents are quite familiar with the Easter candle. We call it our narrative candle, because it tells us about the light and the warmth Jesus has brought among people. No one of us is able, all alone, to give as much light as Jesus did. But if everyone in his or her own way tries to be a little light, all these flames together will be even brighter than the big one of the Easter candle. And that's the way it should be. Jesus hopes his light will be taken over by more and more people. That's why every baptismal candle is always solemnly lit from

the flame of the Easter candle. This way we celebrate the fact
that yet another child has become a light bearer.

From these known symbols we are going to make an effort
to make this difficult feast of Pentecost more meaningful to our
residents. Jesus' life, light, and Spirit are to be continued within
people. First, this happened in his apostles and in Mary; thereafter, it continued further—and now it has reached us.

The Liturgy

We meet in a festively decorated chapel. This day, after all,
is Pentecost, and that's quite something. The burning Easter
candle stands at the center of the chapel, surrounded by more
than a hundred vigil lights arranged like a pyramid fanning
out downwards. Thirteen form the inner circle, symbolizing
the apostles and Mary. A few baptismal candles are put in the
outer, bottom circle. In his opening words, the pastor reminds
everyone of Ascension Day. On that day Jesus went back to
his Father. As the pastor says this, everyone looks up enthusiastically. Pointing his finger upward, one of them exclaims, "Yes, through the clouds!" After Jesus left them, his
friends were very sad. Small wonder! After all, they loved him
very much. How wonderful he was with people! He aroused
their enthusiasm. But what way should they turn now, without him? Certainly, Jesus promised not to let them down, and
he said that he would send a helper, but so far, they hadn't
noticed any support. Today we learn how things turned out!

After making the sign of the cross, we pray for light and
warmth among people, and for all those who are sad or dis-
couraged. Next we read in the Book of God (John 20:19-23).
The pastor continues: "Jesus' friends were gathered together.
They were terrified. They felt like you feel sometimes when
the staff is not around to take care of you. They wondered
about the future. And they were afraid, too. Jesus had been
killed, and that could happen to them, too.

"And then, all of a sudden, there he stood in front of them.
None of them had expected that. 'Peace, don't be afraid!' he
said. 'It's I.' Although he was different now from the way he

was before, Jesus' friends were very glad he was with them again. Jesus wanted to come back once more in order to explain everything to them as thoroughly as possible. And do you know what Jesus did? He breathed on his friends and said: 'Receive my Spirit!' Shall we try to do this, too? Shall I breathe over all of you just like Jesus did?'' The pastor breathes out, very slowly. Through the microphone this is clearly audible. He now asks them to inhale. After a little bit of exercise, it works: The pastor breathes out, and they inhale. "Now, all of you inhale at least a little bit of what I exhale. Jesus also breathed over his friends. And on purpose. His friends needed to partake of his breath, his life. That would help them to become strong. Thus they themselves would be able to do whatever Jesus had shown them.'' Once more the pastor exhales, slowly and quietly. All of them inhale.

Then all of a sudden Ruud stands up. Like a show-off, he shows his muscles. Somewhere along the line he had picked up the word "strong." Whether he has grasped what the story was all about remains an open question. Whatever the case, the leaders as well as the pastor are moved by his performance. The pastor says, "Yes, that's right. That's what happened. Those timid friends all of sudden felt strong again. It was as if all fear had been blown out of them. Now they themselves had to put into practice all that Jesus had been teaching them. They were absolutely convinced that he would help them. Moreover, they felt warmth and ardor again. And that, too, was due to Jesus' presence!

"Now we are going to light the thirteen vigil lights, because they represent the thirteen friends of Jesus. Filled with enthusiasm again, they want to pass on Jesus' light. From now on they are going to continue Jesus' work in his Spirit. Jesus himself can now go back to his Father. We symbolize this by putting out the Easter candle.''

Then we tell them that Jesus' friends threw the doors open. Jesus' good news spread through the town like wildfire. Quite a few people became his followers. More than three thousand, that day alone. "Goh,'' is someone's reaction. The pastor goes on: "What Jesus did while being on earth, we all have to do

now. That's why we light all these lights." Everybody gives
a hand. "That's my light," one says emphatically. This proves
contagious. Now several want to light their own vigil light.
When all the lights are burning, it looks like a pyramid of light.
Fascinated, we look at this beautiful scene.

"Actually, still many more wax lights, or rather, baptismal
candles, should have been put here. Jesus' good news should
not only be spread by you and me, but also by all the children
who are to be baptized. That's why we added these baptismal
candles. They represent the babies who are not born yet."
Close to the lights we pray that we may become a little bit of
light for each other. Next, we go to table for the table prayer.

At the end of the celebration, the pastor reminds everyone
again how the once-timid disciples, after being strengthened
by Jesus' Spirit, threw open the doors and went outside. That's
what we should do, too! Ostentatiously, the doors are opened.
After the blessing, everyone, passing through them, goes
home.

A few thoughtful leaders come and ask for a light for those
who are sick and could not participate. Perhaps we should have
given everyone his or her own light to take home. Whether
the fire department would have liked that idea is quite another
story.

The Light of the Heart

That Sunday we read in the Book of God:
  "You are the light of the world."

Who wants to be a light of the world?
  Who would like to try to be one?
    There are a few who feel like trying.
      Oh, well, how should they know. . . .
    After all, it's always nice
      to be allowed to step forward.

Six come and stand around the book.
  Six lights. That should be sufficient.
The lights of the chapel can be switched off now.
      That's being done.
  Clumsily they stand around the lectern.
      We hardly see anything
    and it's impossible to read.

      For a long time already
    Henk, in the chapel, has been fed up with this tomfoolery.
      He stands up and screams:
  "Of course, that's the light of the heart!"
    He comes forward to explain:
      When we are kind
    we radiate light and warmth,
      light of the heart.
        That's so!

Part II
During the Year

Peace Sunday:
The Animals Tell About God's Peace

Preparation

The longing for peace is a deep-rooted human characteristic. Obviously this also goes for the residents of our home. This yearning for peace is fed by less-peaceful daily experiences. Quarrels about—"I forget the reason!" Anger being released into downright aggression for the simple reason that you weren't understood or someone else was getting it all wrong. Or that urge to be a pest and spoil the atmosphere by getting underfoot, while you are actually longing for cordiality and friendship. Or it is your behavior in general that causes expulsion rather than the confirmation of being a real member of the group. But at times peace does work, and the experience is great.

Our people talk about peace in plain words: "Don't quarrel!" "If you go too far, you have to make up for it!" And indeed, the making-up happens, but it doesn't guarantee lasting peace. Every day one has to search again for ways to put up with each other. That's a tall order! It demands a great deal of ingenuity and endurance from the staff as well as from the residents themselves. This constant search might well be the strongest expression of this stubborn desire for peace.

This threatened but also persistent desire for peace is selected as the subject for our celebration. We look for a story that will not only appeal to the imagination but will also lend itself to being enacted. We opt for Isaiah's portrayal of peace (Isa 11:6-8): The wolf lives with the lamb, the panther lies down with the kid.

As part of the celebration's preparation, we first discuss Isaiah's story with the residents. In the meantime, masks of animals are cut out and colored. Views of how the group feel about the story are exchanged. Some like it very much. That is the way it should be among people, they say, and preferably among animals, too. Others feel Isaiah's depiction isn't realistic.

The creative therapist makes a beautiful big drawing of the story. In the bulletin, all residents are asked to make a mask and to bring it along to the chapel.

The Liturgy

That morning many bring a mask along. They are put on and admired. Everyone looks around and there is a lot of laughter. It's a colorful sight indeed! "It looks like a zoo," someone remarks. The "animals" are sitting next to each other in brotherly fashion. We start with a sign of the cross and sing our peace song.

In his word of welcome the pastor says: "It's Peace Sunday. In all the churches people pray for peace. They ask God to help them because that peace isn't working yet." A number of residents agree. "There is no use praying," one of them yells. They mention the war in the Persian Gulf, and Piet tells about a fight right before going to bed. Some are even pointed at and called by name: "Bert is always looking for trouble." "Geert kicks." "Jan is a sneak!"

The Dog and the Cat

Bert is getting angry. He goes to the pastor and asks him to make them quit teasing. Bert is not wearing a mask. The pastor hands him one. It's one of a dog. Gerard, the one who pointed with his finger, swaps his mask. Now he is wearing that of a cat. He too comes forward. There they are, standing opposite each other, a cat and a dog. The pastor remarks: "A cat and a dog aren't friends. They often fight, scare each other, and make each other angry. These two animals show us how people, and we ourselves, very often behave."

Kees, peaceful by nature, screams, "Make up for it!" He stands between them, but the cat and the dog won't listen. As so often in the past, his peace effort fails. He gives the pastor a questioning look. This situation is beginning to weigh down on him as well as on the others. Arie screams that the staff or the pastor himself should help. The pastor tells Kees and Arie: "Come and stand next to Bert and Gerard. You may be able to help them." Arie goes to Hans, a group leader, who also joins them.

Dog Bert and Cat Gerard show clearly that there is no peace. Kees and Arie make it clear that their attitude isn't right, but they feel helpless and ask for help.

The Wolf and the Rabbit

Next Henk comes forward. He explains that foxes eat rabbits, as happened not too long ago at the children's farm. Foxes are mean animals! Although wearing a mask of a wolf, he catches Roel, a "rabbit" to demonstrate how foxes act. The poor "victim" runs off behind the altar and starts crying that Henk has hurt him.

Henk raises his mask and looks dismayed. It wasn't meant like that. "I am Henk, not the wolf," he says to Roel. He doesn't want to be taken for a wolf or be called mean all the time. Henk is not the only one who hears, very often, "You are nothing but . . . " No, he is more, he is Henk, extending a hand. But Roel doesn't notice. Most likely, he does not expect it. The pastor asks who is able to help Henk and Roel. Henk points to Marjan, his group leader, his help and support. Marjan strokes Henk's hair and goes to Roel. She helps him to seize Henk's hand.

Siem and the Lion

Meanwhile there is a lot going on in front of and around the altar. Henk and Roel make peace. Between Gerard and Bert the effort fails. Gerard is willing all right, but Bert has been too much hurt. In the chapel, still other "animals" are looking on, seriously or playfully. For instance, Siem, in his wheelchair, isn't wearing a mask but sits comfortably next to Mia, a "lion." The pastor points to them, saying: "Siem and the lion are getting along fine. Siem isn't afraid of the lion, and the lion does not eat him up!"

"I know Mia for a long time already," Siem says. "She may act a little surly at times, but she is really very nice! " He takes off her mask and says, "You see?" And now the pastor tells the others what Siem did. He took off Mia's mask. She isn't just a surly lion, no, not at all, she is nice, too. That is the way for all of us to be well off together.

Gijs Restores Bert's Prestige

Ron is walking through the chairs taking off masks here and there. It's an act, but it gives him a feeling of relief. Bert, meanwhile, isn't relaxed yet. He is still angry. The pastor asks Kees to take off Bert's mask, just like Siem did for Mia. Then he asks, "Is Bert nothing but a troublemaker, or is there something worth telling about him?" Gijs, who is also using a wheelchair, says that Bert wheels him very often and that he would not like to be without him. Bert's face brightens, and he comes and sits down next to Gijs.

Isaiah's Peace Vision

In the meantime, nearly everyone has changed places. Some are sitting on chairs, others are sitting on the floor around the altar. Most of them have taken off their masks. Once more the pastor recounts what happened a few minutes ago and mentions all the people who were needed to restore peace. Next, he points to the drawing depicting Isaiah's peace vision and tells the story of God's peace promise (Isa 11:6-8).

We light the Easter candle, Jesus' peace light for us. Then we sing a song about the Good Shepherd.

Communion

Next to the masks, our examples of violence and vulnerability, the plate with hosts and the cup of wine are put on the altar table. They are the symbols of Jesus' presence, God's own peace promise. Around Jesus differences are bridged, and the hope for peace is kept alive. Everyone is welcome to his table.

Together we thank God for sending Jesus to teach us peace. For that peace we pray. We also pray that there will always be people like Hans, Marjan, Arie, Kees, and Siem, who have been helping us make up for what was wrong. We also ask the Lord for more people like them. Gijs prays for Bert. Then a prayer follows for President Bush and for people at war. We give thanks for the "animals," who showed us what God's peace is like. Then, together, we pray the Our Father and sing a Communion song. While distributing Holy Communion, the pastor calls each person by name and says, "Bert, Jan, Carla, . . . you are called to peace in Jesus' name."

By shaking hands, we wish one another peace. After asking God's blessing, everybody goes home.

World Pet's Day:
The Guinea Pig on the Altar

Preparation

Peace Sunday is followed by the celebration of World Pet's Day. In last week's celebration, too, animals were involved. In Isaiah's peace vision, they showed how peaceful relations among people should be. Little by little our residents are discovering that in the story of God and humankind, animals play an important role. They are, after all, in their own way narrator's of God's plan. That's why they deserve our respect and care.

Saint Francis of Assisi was deeply convinced of that. Proofs are his *Canticle of the Sun* and the legends that are told about him. On the fourth of October, which is also World Pet's Day, the liturgy should not be celebrated without animals. On this day we consider them as being our peers in God's creation. God created humans and animals and we, his children, are allowed to enjoy having them. In addition, these animals mobilize our attention and carefulness.

In a home like ours, there are many animals, not only on the children's farm but also in the home itself. On World Pet's Day everyone is allowed to take his own pet along to the chapel. And that's what happens.

The Liturgy

That morning, a large assortment of animals fills the chapel. There are canaries and parakeets in their cages. There are two guinea pigs, a cat and a rabbit, white mice, goldfish, even a kid. Those who don't have a pet bring their cuddle toy along. All in all, a colorful collection.

A welcome song that mentions animals in one of its stanzas opens the celebration. Next, the pastor shows a picture of Saint Francis surrounded by animals. He is talking to them. Some of those present discover their own animal in the drawing. They are invited to talk about it—what it is called, what food it needs, how it has to be taken care of, what it is afraid of. Johan says that his dog is scared when there is a thunderstorm. Gerard, who has brought along white mice, asks Herman to keep his cat in the box. Herman's immediate reaction: "My cat doesn't do anything like that." Piet shows his guinea pig. It is called Puk, and it eats a lot of green leaves. In fact, no sooner does Piet put his guinea pig on the altar than it starts nibbling on the leaf of a plant that has been put there. Nic doesn't like that. He is working in the garden, and that offends his pride. He cries, "Get that animal out of here!" This yelling frightens Piet, and he snatches Puk away. "Well," says Nic, trying to make things better, "tomorrow I'll bring another plant."

It's moving to see how they praise their animals, how proud they are of them, how they protect and take care of them. And how they are loved by their pets. We sing a song of thanks.

The pastor tells about Saint Francis. He was a real animal lover and urged everyone to be careful about animals. After all, God himself cares for them and has made them our helpers and friends. Puk, the guinea pig, is still on the altar. Piet stands next to it. He makes it clear to the pastor that a prayer should be said for Puk, too. That's done—but not only for Puk. The rabbit, the parakeets, the white mice, and the goldfish— all of them are now put on the altar table. We bring them before God to show him our gratitude for them. The intercessory prayer is an unusual one this time but, without any doubt, sincere and wholehearted.

God provides for humans and animals. God takes care of all of them. That's why the pastor puts a bowl containing some food for each animal on the altar table: a few leaves of lettuce, seed for the birds, some fish food. For the cuddle toys there is a ribbon. Before each animal is taken back, it gets something from the bowl. We sing the animal name song. In conclusion, the pastor prays for all the residents, as he thanks them for their good care and asks God's blessing on these good caretakers of his creation.

After praying the Our Father together, we end the service with a song.

All Saints' Day, All Souls' Day

Preparation

Late in the fall, we celebrate the feasts of Saint Martin and Saint Nicholas, no strangers to our residents. Both feasts have their own folklore and customs, and are celebrated in our homes with much festivity. And for good reason. The memory of these two saints inspires a desire in people to perform good deeds. It also keeps hope alive. But that's not the only reason for a feast. In addition to Saint Martin and Saint Nicholas, there are other saints who are very familiar to our people. They know the saints for whom they are named. They know that the chapel bears the name of Saint Joseph or Saint Ursula. Some of the older ones still remember the monastic names of the Brothers or Sisters who used to take care of them.

We want to celebrate All Saints' Day in the precious memory of all those holy people and all who are named after them: Brothers, Sisters, fathers, mothers, good friends, acquaintances. Some of them have died, others are still alive. All of them have one thing in common: They were, or they still are, kind to our residents. They brought a little bit of heaven on earth or, at least, kept hope alive. Quite often, our residents take pictures of them along to the chapel and want to pray for them.

Thus, All Saints' Day and All Souls' Day belong together. They are a celebration of the community of saints in heaven and on earth.

The Liturgy

There are quite a few pictures of saints on and around the altar table. There are statues of Saint Joseph, Mary, and Saint Anthony. There are icons of Peter and Paul and a picture of Lourdes with Bernadette and Mary. In addition there are pictures of Saint Nicholas and Saint Francis, a statue of Saint Martin riding a horse with a beggar next to it. Finally, the statue of Jesus, the Good Shepherd.

Added to this collection are pictures of family members and residents who have passed away. The pastor has brought the icons and Saint Martin's statue; all the others belong to the residents.

Some saints are immediately identified. With others, they try to find out who they are. The pastor introduces by name all the saints represented on the altar. "How do you become a saint?" he asks. Nico seems to know the answer: Saint Nicholas is a saint because he brings presents. Saint Martin because he cut his coat in two, sharing one part with a beggar. "And Mary is a saint because she was a good mother, wasn't she?" Piet asks. The names of many saints are mentioned. The pastor tells something about each one of them. He also points out that our own names remind us of saints. Thus Piet is derived from Petrus, Riet from Mary, Marga from Margaretha, and Toon from Antonius.

The pastor explains that saints are people who see at once what will benefit others. They are prepared to do everything when it comes to helping people. In this sense, they are good in the same way that God is good. It's a blessing just to meet them. Small wonder, then, that people such as the beggar of Saint Martin's and all those receiving presents feel happy and cheerful. "A feast," calls Toon. Yes, they bring a little bit of heaven to people—they bring heaven to earth. And that's a feast!

It Looks Like a Feast

The Easter candle, our Jesus light, stands next to the altar. Jesus was a light for people. Saints act just like him, and that's why they are God's friends. They are his lights, too. That's the reason that a festive vigil light is put in front of every picture of a saint. This light is lit by a small candle, which in turn got its light from the Easter candle.

The vigil lights in front of the pictures of fathers, mothers, and acquaintances aren't lit, yet. The picture of Jan's father stands on the altar table. "My father is in heaven," says Jan. He is asked to tell something about his father. Jan tells how, at home or when his father came to visit him, they went out for a ride together and how they had some cake on the way. Jan had a good father. He now lives in heaven, and it is Jan's deep conviction that his father is as great a saint as all the others. And so, he comes forward and lights a vigil light in front of his father's picture.

That proves infectious. Others follow his example. And whether they took along a photo or not, we listen to their stories and we light a vigil light. Fathers, mothers, and friends still among us are called, and group leaders aren't forgotten either. Soon a lot of light is shining, and we almost run out of room.

"It looks like a feast!" Nico says. Siem mentions Bert, who very often wheels his wheelchair. Bert is holy, too. At this remark, Bert beams. Very often he has heard just the opposite. The pastor invites everyone to have a look at Bert: He is a light himself, a light for Siem. It's a moving sight: so many vigil lights standing for as many—sometimes difficulty expressed—memories. These small lights reveal the presence of ordinary saints bringing heaven on earth sometimes, for a moment. They are sorely needed to keep up courage. Really, it looks like a feast!

Thus, people, each in his or her own way, bring to life once again the communion of saints in heaven and on earth. They feel like being members of that community.

We sing still another song and pray the intercessory prayer. In conclusion, the pastor prays to all the saints in heaven to commend to God their namesakes on earth. Petrus should not forget all *de Pieten*—all the Peters—neither Saint Francis all *de Fransen.*

Then we pray the Our Father. On the altar table we make room for the plate with hosts and the cup of wine. "Thus Jesus remains with us and makes us holy," the pastor says. Next, we go to Communion.

Thijs has brought along his recorder and Herman his mouth organ, and now they ask permission to play. Their performance enhances the final part of the service. In conclusion, we sing a song and pray God to bless all of us.

No More Pain

All of you saw it yourselves:
   Leo's body became ill, weak.
    His body couldn't take it any longer.
And like a plant that is drooping its leaves and dies,
  so Leo's body died, too.
    But Leo himself,
  Leo who loved us, and lived with us,
   his own "ego" stays now with God our Father.
  We believe that he is very happy over there,
   with no more pain.
  In heaven Leo stays with his own mother, too.

You See This Woman?

Preparation

In this Sunday's Gospel, the story is about the woman who sprinkles Jesus' feet with her tears and dries them with her hair. Simon, a Pharisee whose guest Jesus is, notices what happens and gets annoyed. After all, this woman is a sinner and has a bad reputation. Jesus, however, says to Simon, "Just look at this woman with different eyes. And then what's your conclusion?"

How do you look at someone else? What do you want to see? Do you only have an eye for what's bad, or do you also see the good traits? These questions are going to be the main topics of this and next weekend's services. Our residents don't hold back from calling each other names once in a while or giving each other the cold shoulder. In these celebrations we want to invite them to look at each other the way Jesus did. He saw what was good in the woman when everyone else had only an eye for her bad deeds. Jesus didn't stigmatize her because of her past.

The Liturgy

When we enter the chapel this morning, we see brightly colored signs hanging all over the place. On them, terms of abuse: liar, thief, sneak, glutton, bawler, wrangler, stinker. One even carries the word "whore." Most of our people can't read. And those who are able to have great difficulty reading. Every time they succeed in figuring out what's on the sign, embarrassed laughter can be heard: "Words like that don't belong in a chapel, do they?"

Even the management and visitors from outside are reading the signs with mixed feelings: "What's on the program now? Is a whore going to be today's subject? And with these residents?"

In his word of welcome the pastor mentions the fact that nearly all the terms of abuse painted on the signs can, now and then, be heard in our home. That's what we are going to talk about together. In the Book of God we find a story about someone who was always scolded and who always got the cold shoulder. Later on in the service we are going to read this story.

As usual, we open the celebration with a sign of the cross, and we think for a moment, in silence, of God our Father. Then we pray the opening prayer.

This Sunday's story is told. "Do you know how this woman was hooted at?" the pastor asks. "They called her a whore." "Bad," someone calls out. Obviously, no one is familiar with the word "whore." The pastor leaves it at that and writes the word "bad" on the blackboard. One by one he reads the other abuse words on the signs and asks them whether they can mention still more expressions of this kind. Well, yes, they can. Some of the visitors are really a little embarrassed. "Who of you ever told a lie?" asks the pastor. At first no one answers. But then someone is exposed! He comes forward and the sign "liar" is hung around his neck. Another one gets the sign "wrangler," a third one, "thief."

Some chuckling can be heard. So far the labeled ones don't seem to suffer much under their fate. They even seem to enjoy it. The matter alters, however, as soon as the pastor hides them behind a curtain and says, "Good riddance to bad rubbish. We don't want to have anything to do with liars, wranglers, and thieves!"

The "liar" emerges from behind the curtain and grasps the pastor. He wants to belong. "He doesn't lie all the time, he is nice, too," someone calls out from the chapel. All the others are called back, too. "It must be awful being called a liar all the time and having nobody around who knows something good about you. And that's what happened to the woman in the story we have told you. Everyone called her bad. She had left her husband." Some of them show that they know what we are talking about. Their parents are separated, too. "Nobody first asked what exactly had happened, and how it all had come about. No, immediately they hung a sign around her neck. She became an outcast without even a chance to learn from her mistakes and do better again. Was that women really that bad?"

"In Jesus' eyes she was also a nice woman," André calls out from the chapel. "Exactly, André. Jesus knew she was also a kind woman, because he looked at her heart. He saw that she also had a good side and that she was able to be very good and kind!"

A short discussion with the three labeled ones follows. "Would you like to walk around with such a sign? Would you like to be looked upon as just a liar, a wrangler, or a thief?" No, they wouldn't. One already has taken off his sign. Together we search for their good sides, the way they helped others and shared with them. The signs are torn apart. Everybody heaves a sigh of relief. It was, without doubt, a little exciting. The three "victims" are called to table. After all, there is room for everyone who is good at heart and of good will, even though, once in a while, they make mistakes. The torn-up signs are lying on a pile in front of the altar. To reach the table, one has to go around them. Together we celebrate Mass.

At the end of the celebration, everyone is urged to pay special attention in the next week to each other's good traits. All residents receive a sheet of sturdy cardboard on which a heart is drawn. This can be cut out and hung around the neck. An explanation is added: "Write on the heart all you appreciate in another."

Thus, the "sermon" goes home.

Peter Is a Fibber

Preparation

On this Sunday in June, we celebrate the feast of Saint Peter. Today, last week's theme will be elaborated upon a little further. Everybody is invited to come to the chapel with his "heart" around his neck. During the week, extra hearts have been sent to those who weren't able to attend the previous celebration.

It's such glorious weather that we celebrate this feast in the open. We meet on the lawn behind the chapel.

The Liturgy

After opening the service, the pastor tells the story of Saint Peter. While he is doing this, one of those present comes and stands next to him. He will act the role of Peter. In the same way as in the celebration last Sunday, Peter gets a few labels stuck on. One of the residents in the chapel calls Peter a hothead. The one playing the role of Peter is so wrapped up in the story that he himself offers a pungent characterization of Saint Peter. In his opinion Peter is a fibber, because he told the soldiers he didn't know Jesus. Two characterizations, "hothead" and "fibber" are written on the sign hanging around Peter's neck. That even Peter is a fibber apparently puts the mind of someone present at rest. Beaming, he tells his atten-

84

dant, "Well, Peter told lies, too. Peter told a fib, too. That's what the pastor says, isn't it?"

Peter may be a hothead and a fibber, but that's no reason for Jesus to let him down. Jesus saw much more in Peter. To demonstrate this, we turn Peter's sign around. Then, the pastor takes it off and tears it up, just the way we did last week.

Now the pastor hangs a heart around Peter's neck. After all, Peter did have a good heart. Jesus called him "rock," which means "you can lean on me."

Upon hearing these words, Peter shows his muscle. Seeing this, Freek, who is deaf, jumps on Peter's back. It's a concrete demonstration of what it means to be a tower of strength for someone else. Jesus also called Peter "shepherd." Our people are familiar with the concept of "shepherd"; it was explained to them at length in connection with the story about the Good Shepherd. "Rock" and "shepherd" are the two words written on Peter's heart. One of the attendants adds a drawing.

We now focus our attention on the others' hearts. Many come forward to have the pastor read what was written on them. Some want to get another blank one. The attendants' hearts, too, are picked up. The fact that only a few have brought theirs along indicates that apparently something hasn't clicked. Obviously, most of them do not feel like participating.

We agree to take some more time to write down each other's good traits. The group leaders aren't forgotten either. It's a moving and fascinating happening—it inspires confidence and strengthens at the same time. That's headway!

Some of the residents' hearts turn out to be blank because no one knows much about them. "Who knows something nice about Hans and Jaak?" the pastor asks. It's quiet for a moment. Then a girl comes forward and says, "When I am coming from work, Jaak sometimes supports me." She draws a little circle on Jaak's heart.

We pray the intercessory prayers, sing a song of thanks, and celebrate Mass. At Communion time, the pastor sees quite a few hearts passing by. Everyone goes home with a heart completely filled up. There, it continues to work. Some of them keep on walking around with their hearts for the rest of the week. Others come knocking on the door letting me know that, once again, someone—the therapy leader, a brother, the one in charge of the night shift, a fellow resident—has written something on his heart. One of them has his group's photo stuck on it.

A married couple who attended the service and were deeply moved calls. They mention how they, too, told each other what traits they appreciate in the other. They have written them down in a kind of love letter to each other. By "home mail," the pastor also receives a cut-out heart. On it: "Thanks very much for the wonderful service and the way you care for our residents."

Real Love Has a Price

Preparation

The things people come up with to tell each other "I love you"! They buy flowers, perfume, or other expensive presents. Quite often our residents make drawings for their parents and the administration. Rarely do they go home without taking some flowers along. And should they forget, the attendants see to it that flowers are part of their luggage.

It's important to demonstrate time and again that we love each other. This is the theme we will dwell on in this service. Of course, this topic would fit extremely well on a day like Mother's Day. But why not on just an ordinary Sunday? After all, you don't need to wait for a special day in order to show your love for another. But for us, this Sunday's circumstances prove favorable, because after the home's Jubilee, the chapel is still richly decorated with flowers.

The Liturgy

We meet in that festively decorated chapel. Lots of flowers indicate that there has been a big feast. It's nice to donate flowers. It's wonderful when you see you are making someone happy with them. And it is also great when you yourself receive flowers or a gift.

Jesus feels the same way. Today a story from the Book of God tells us more about that. After the sign of the cross and the opening prayer, the pastor tells the story. It's about a woman pouring precious nard balm over Jesus' head.

Just Smell: He/She Loves Me

"Who of you ever gets some nice-smelling perfume?" A faint giggle is the first reaction to the pastor's question. Then a girl raises her finger and says, "I—from Piet." Laughter resounds. The pastor takes the girl under his protection. "It's wonderful to have a lovely scent, isn't it? Actually, you can smell that Piet loves you." Now more fingers are raised, and boys start telling about the aftershave they got from Mom or their girlfriend on their birthdays.

Next, we dwell for a moment upon the grumbling Pharisee. He thinks it is a shame about that money! Jesus says, "The poor you have always with you, but not me." Of course, the poor do have to be taken care of. But always for the love of Christ. And when it comes to loving Christ, what's money? How wonderful Jesus must smell! That woman loves him. And Jesus doesn't object. He is only too pleased.

Just Smell: God Our Father Loves Me

In the Bible we find still another story about having a lovely odor. According to the Book of God, God our Father will provide us with a heavenly odor after we have died and are with him in heaven. Then, he will anoint our heads just like Jesus' head was anointed by the woman. This way, he will show us that he loves us.

"How about doing right now what God is going to do when we meet him?" Generously, we sprinkle fragrant perfume on the heads of our altar boys. It smells great, but not everyone is able to smell it, and so the acolytes are asked to walk into the chapel. In absolute silence, everybody smells their fragrant heads. "Just smell," the acolytes say. "God our Father loves me."

As soon as they have returned, we pray. We thank God our Father for all the people who love us. We express our hope that we'll never give others a cold shoulder. After all, we need each other. We also ask that we may always be able to make presents for one another.

Then we go to table. The altar boys, still sweet-smelling, come and stand beside the pastor. Once more he reminds everyone of what is written in the Book of God. After we have died, our Father will love to have us with him. He will anoint us and invite us to come to his table, where he himself will serve us. Whether the residents are able to understand this remains to be seen. Still, for the pastor and the leaders, this biblical image is a poignant one. Already now, we celebrate what awaits us in the future. That image is as vivid as the fragrance of the altar boys that surrounds us.

After the blessing, quite a few residents come forward to have their heads sprinkled with perfume, also. Sweet-smelling, they return home. There, the leaders who weren't able to attend the service are in for it! "Just smell, God loves me!" What in the world happened in the chapel this time? We better find out . . .

Let People Smell That You Are Baptized

It's a big feast, every time we are baptizing a baby in our chapel.
Generously we anoint it with fragrant chrism,
    because later on this little child will have to spread
    Christ's good scent.
After the anointing, everybody may come and smell.
    Let us hope that once this child has grown up
    we will be able to smell by its behavior
    that it was baptized today.

Just for a Short While, Heaven on Earth

Preparation

It is something that really keeps our residents preoccupied: A relative, or sometimes a coresident, passes away. "Where is papa now?" they ask. What are you going to tell them? "Papa is with God our Father." What it is like, how it might be . . . you just start stammering. And yet, the Bible offers quite a few images. We look them over and select Psalm 23. It's delightfully concrete and therefore best suited to helping our residents "experience" heaven. Don't we, after all, experience a little bit of heaven every time we are kind to one another? Heaven might be just like that experience: fellowship, being welcome, having no more pain, a feast!

To Meadows of Green Grass He Leads Me

Thus we wait for a very summery day and come together on the "meadows of green grass" next to the chapel. The residents head through a festive gate of posts to which hundreds of balloons have been attached. We anoint their heads with cologne and welcome them with a sweet-smelling flower. They come and sit down around the fountain, with its serene, murmuring water. The soft music of bells resounds in the background.

The entrance procession is extra festive. In front, six acolytes, followed by boys and girls with two hundred balloons. Spontaneously, the residents get up, and on the beat of their applause, a solemn entry is made. After the procession the balloons are used as a festive background to the altar table.

The Liturgy

The pastor welcomes everybody: "I am glad to see you. How festive you look! And the sun, how wonderful! Just let's forget that sulky weather, and all quarrels and all that's annoying. We want to make up for those things and bring a little bit of heaven on earth by being glad with one another. Have a good look at each other and shake hands with each another. And if you feel like it, just say, 'I am glad to see you.' " They do shake hands. Next, we make a sign of the cross. God our Father belongs first of all to our family.

Now it becomes quiet. We listen to the murmuring water and have the sun warm our faces. Then we pray: "God our Father, thank you for this beautiful spot. Thank you for the wonderful green grass, the sun on our faces, and the fresh water. How nice we are allowed to be here. We thank you for giving us each other. How great, so many people are loving us. How wonderful, you want to love us. Today we want to enjoy it all. Amen."

Photos of Those Who Have Passed Away

The pastor continues: "You have brought along photos, haven't you? Just show them to me. Raise them. Who are they?" Names are called. "Where are they now?" "In heaven with God," someone calls.

Now the pastor takes the Bible in his hands and says, "We have looked in the Holy Book of God to find out what heaven would be like. And I discovered that it might be something like we enjoy here this morning—green grass, fresh water, and cologne on your head. In heaven, you can smell that God loves you. And there, we are going to meet our daddies and mommies again." Other names are called. The pastor says, "Please put all the photos on the altar table." After that is done, the pictures are decorated with fresh flowers.

No More Pain

"Some of these people had a long spell of sickness. Their bodies said, No! Do you still remember . . . and . . . of section X? But in heaven there will be no more pain. When you are tired of being ill, when you have had lots of grief, when you aren't able to walk—all this will be gone in heaven, and wheelchairs won't be needed any longer."

Next, all of them are sprinkled with fresh water from the fountain—water, a source of life that rejuvenates. We eat toast with real honey. The bitterness of life is gone; all these things remind us of the land of honey. The sprinkling with water is real; we feel its wetness. Together, we express this in song: "Be quiet, just wait, everything will be new."

One of the residents comes and sits down next to the small band of musicians. He always walks around with a toy saxophone, and sometimes he plays during the services in his own manner and completely off-key. Today he joins the band as if he were an accomplished musician. And all of a sudden it dawns on the pastor: In heaven he most likely will play his instrument like a professional.

He Put a Child in the Midst of Them

Then we stage the story of the children who weren't allowed to come to Jesus. This has to be done in a concrete manner. The fellow workers try to get Jesus' (the role of the pastor) attention. They think the world of themselves. After all, they are rich. They know the Book of God by heart and therefore consider themselves to be real friends of Jesus. One of the residents thinks otherwise. He comes forward and screams, "You have to share!"

The pastor takes over: "Look what Jesus did." After all the bickering about who is the greatest in the kingdom of God, he brushes all these "important" people aside and puts a child in a wheelchair in the middle of the circle. "Don't you see that you are standing in this child's way? Just let this child come into the circle!"

Next he tells something about this child: How she has undergone numerous operations, and how she has always been cheerful. We lay hands on the child and say, "God loves you."

We invite the attendants to lay their hands on the heads of those entrusted to their care. There is some hesitation. Some do, some don't. But still, they manifest something of God's kindness. We sing "Let the Children Come to Me."

He Serves Me at Table

Then we go to the festively decorated table, and pray a table prayer. Communion is distributed. They may drink of either the wine or grape juice, fruit of the grape vine.

We sing "If You Don't Love Each Other." Next, we thank God our Father: "Thank you for this gathering and this meal. It will keep us going for a while. Help us and strengthen us on our way to your heavenly meal, and bless us."

We conclude the service in a festive manner. Everybody gets up from his or her seat. Music resounds. We want to proclaim everywhere that there is real hope for a little bit of heaven and peace on earth. To send this message into the world, some thirty pigeons are released. The residents have brought along greeting cards, colored beforehand. On the front is the text: "When people are really nice to each other, a little bit of heaven comes down on earth." On the back there's room for a personal message. The group leaders help the residents write their messages, and the cards are attached to the balloons. The trumpet plays "When the Saints," and we dance together. Then, as the trumpets play, the balloons take to the air, announcing that there is real hope for a little bit of heaven and peace on earth.

In any case, we are able to experience this, this morning.

Looking Back

The celebration lasts, all in all, one hour. The time goes quickly. Afterward, management and visitors discuss their experience for quite a while. The residents don't—they just enjoyed it. For them, it was one big feast. From the sections we learn how they have kept on talking about the balloons and the child in the wheelchair. Maybe they have grasped that heaven means that God gives you a hearty welcome, that it is something like real community: a feast. Gradually we have come to realize the impact this service has had on our own selves. Having one's head anointed, eating honey, reviving the memories of those who have passed away, putting a child in the middle of the group, laying—daring to lay—hands on, all these concrete moves—our residents needed them, but how realistic a Christian experience they were even for us: pastor, management, visitors.

Only much later do we realize that this service looked very much like the meal mentioned in the Gospel, for which people are brought together from the corners and the streets, and where the "saxophonist," the cripple, and the blind alike choose their own places. It was the gospel vividly experienced in our life. It was heaven, just for a short while.

Part III
Special Celebrations

When Words Fail

The intellectual faculties of most of our residents are very limited. In addition, quite a few also suffer from multiple physical handicaps. Crippled for life, they are confined to bed or wheelchair, and all their lives, they have to be attended to. Most of them aren't able to speak, and only very attentive attendants succeed in grasping the meaning of the sounds they utter. These people live in pavilions equipped with special facilities. One of them is called Golden Rain.

It is primarily through their senses that these residents experience the outside world. They intensely enjoy light and darkness and the taste, smell, sound, and sense of all things they get in touch with. But they can also get upset by these experiences. Dealing with them demands a great deal of love and patience. Tempo must be low. One must always be fully aware of what exactly one wants to communicate. It can easily become too much or too fussy. And in that case they become easily confused. Endlessly they may be occupied with a toy, play with a rattle, or repeat one motion again and again.

Those who visit them need courage to step into their world. In their presence one feels uneasy, and it is hard to decide on one's attitude toward them. All kinds of contradictory feelings flash through the mind: feelings of aversion and, at the same time, of pity and sadness. Then, too, there is a sense of anger deep within the heart, resentment that some people are forced to live with that kind of handicap.

Those who are courageous enough to join them learn to interpret their world. You come to interpret their gestures and sounds; you learn to love them the way they are. In dealing with these people, it isn't accomplishment that counts. There is not much that can be done. Most important is being available. And not even that always goes easily or smoothly.

To enable our residents to unwind once in a while, a special room, called the Whisper Room, is available. In there, they can enjoy light effects or the sensation of wind blowing through their hair. Others may enjoy listening to music or touching different kinds of objects.

Dealing with them in their world entails that we, for our part, become more conscious in our way of sensing, looking, and listening. The "healthy world," where achievement, skill, and knowledge are the only things that count, is put into perspective. Rarely do people have time, and therefore many beautiful things are often missed. In contrast, our residents only want us to be around. As far as they are concerned, not that much has to be achieved. Even so, if you want to succeed in getting along with them, it will be necessary to become a different person.

"God Our Father Loves Them, Too"

Sometimes, the residents of Golden Rain attend the service along with us, some more than others. Most of the time the leaders know whether these residents like being there or not. Some of them crow with pleasure when a young people's choir adds luster to the service. All that's new is intensely absorbed by them. But it also happens that they become frightened, bored, or start yelling. In that case, some intervention may be necessary in order to continue the service. When, some time ago, some older residents were asked whether this kind of disturbance was bothering them, one of them, highly indignant, replied, "God our Father loves them, too. When they always have to stay in their section, no one knows anymore that they belong here, too."

Sometimes the theme of the service is focused on them in a special way. In that case, quite a bit of creativity is needed.

After all, words are useless to them. Most important is to create an atmosphere in which they feel at ease.

As for ourselves, these kind of services are very moving. It makes us feel good, being with them in God our Father's space: everyone the way he or she is. For our part, we, with our love for them, our impatience, our helplessness, our questions. All of us united in God, with and for each other. From this background, the following services originated.

Cuddle Sunday

Preparation

On this Sunday our residents are invited to come to the chapel and bring their cuddle toys along. A very special invitation is sent to the residents of Golden Rain. Bearing in mind that this group doesn't have much use for words, we have composed, this time, a service just for them.

The chapel is attractive; the lighting subdued. Lying around the altar are mattresses, hassocks, and blankets. Big cuddle toys have been put between them. Attendants and a few parents shuffle along with their "children." All have their cuddle toy or doll with them. Everyone is looking for a comfortable spot. The smaller ones are sitting in their attendants' laps. The others, depending on their handicap, are lying down or half-sitting.

Apparently the sounds of the music therapist's guitar and her quiet singing voice are recognized. These lovely sounds are calming. And all of a sudden it dawns on us that this scenery in our chapel very much resembles what Mark describes in his Gospel (6:56): "They laid the sick in the marketplaces."

The pastor walks through all this commotion, here and there gently stroking a child's hair. Then he bids them all welcome. Those in wheelchairs, their cuddle toys "on board," pull closer. One by one, the pastor must admire their "little friends." One of the residents comes, dragging along his "Uncle James." It's nearly five feet tall. Uncle James, too, finds a spot on the floor.

The Liturgy

The pastor opens the service with a hearty welcome. Solemnly, we make a sign of the cross. Then we pray. ''God our Father, here we are together with many residents who don't meet here very often. They don't know very much about you, but we believe that you know them very well. You love everyone the way he or she was born. Together, we just want to spend an enjoyable time with you, who loves us so much. Be close to us during this hour, so that we may feel your presence in our hearts. Amen.''

One of the attendants is sitting in a rocking chair. With her are the residents of her section, all armed with their cuddle toys and busy talking about the topics they usually discuss with their ''friends.'' The attendants claim that a cuddle toy not only ''understands'' them but also has a calming effect on them.

The service continues with this song: ''I and my cuddle toy. With it, I am feeling better. Life is nicer with my cuddle toy around.'' It's a familiar song. They rock and clap to the rhythm. The atmosphere is pleasant, and judging from the racket they make, our residents are having a good time. For the Golden Rain residents, the music therapist has composed a special song. Accompanied by her guitar, a little girl with a beautiful voice starts singing it:

> Golden Rainchild just listen to the wind.
> Listen to my playing and try to sense what I want to tell you.
> Words you don't understand,
> but that little voice you won't forget.
> It is as if you really see me,
> and you are glad having me around again.
> Sometimes I don't know what you want to tell me,
> because so often, you are so calm, so quiet.
> I feel so helpless, sometimes,
> and in that moment of powerlessness,
> I wonder whether you are happy then.
>
> Golden Rainchild, sometimes you are as old as I am.
> The child within you, is just like me,
> we don't differ that much.

I like to be cuddled, even though I feel pain at times.
I too want to be happy.
I am just an ordinary human being too, just like you.
Yet I don't understand what you want to tell me then,
even though you often are so calm and quiet.
Are you in that telling-moment, what I think, still happy then?
Even though you aren't able to talk, you are telling me
    so much sometimes.
But even though I do my utmost,
and there still is something left for me:
you then give yourself, the way you feel.
Perhaps that's my problem: that I don't dare to be
    the way I feel inside.

Golden Rainchild I just listen to the wind.
I watch your game
and sense what you want to tell me.
You words I don't understand,
but that little voice I won't forget.
It is, as if I am now seeing again, being glad we are
    now together.
And only now, I understand what you want to tell me then,
even though I look so calm and quiet
and feel restless in such a moment then.
Is it this that you want to tell me:
I am a human being after all?

> (Frits Schoerent and Don McLean, "Vincent")

Expressed in this song, pastors, parents, and attendants are hearing the feelings they so often experience during their daily tasks. That's why the song is so moving, giving them food for thought.

During these quiet moments, one of the leaders tells the story of Nicodemus, the story of the man who, in the middle of the night, went to Jesus to share with him what he had on his mind (John 3). Then the pastor, surrounded by mattresses, wheelchairs, and animals, gives a short meditation. Among other things, he says: "For safety and security, our people look to their cuddle animals. With them they share their disappointments and the things they enjoy. They talk to them in order to come to terms with themselves. Nicodemus, too, needed to talk to someone about all he had on his mind: the pain, the grief, and the desires deep down in his heart. And in the safety and security of the night, he looks for Jesus. By day, he is the confident leader, but by night he is the man who lies awake. Jesus recognizes his heart's desire: the dream of a different world. How wonderful if we, too, could get help from one another, be accepted by people who are trying to understand us. Just like these residents bringing us down to the level of an ordinary person, asking us straight out: 'Love me!' ''

After some more music, we pray for patience with and sympathy for all these residents who are teaching us to be human. We pray that we may always be a source of safety and security for each other. A short table service follows. At the part of the service where we wish each other peace, the attendants are invited to give ''their children'' a kiss or a sign of the cross. While soft music resounds and a lot of mumbling can be heard from our people, we go to Communion. We pray: ''God our Father, it is wonderful being with you the way we are. Thus we find each other from heart to heart, and probably understand what you had in mind: a table where vulnerable people and people in need are really welcome. Be so kind and bless all of us. Amen.''

Looking Back

The service has taken place on different levels—on that of the residents and on that of ours. It was just wonderful being with God that way. Children's services may be useful, but a service where children are sitting in the laps of their attendants can be an especially wonderful experience. Other cultures have fewer problems with that. When Indian children in Canada start yelling during a service, their mothers just solve the problem by nursing them. You won't see that happening in our areas very often.

In any case, Cuddle Sunday carries us a step further on the way toward a Church where human feelings count again.

I Put My Bow in the Clouds

Preparation

A large rainbow hangs against the chapel's rear wall. In a previous celebration we talked about Noah—how God our Father wanted to mark the beginning of a new era with him. What had happened never would happen again. Never again would the power of water be so devastating. This God promised, and as a sign of his covenant with humankind, he put in the clouds a bow, like protective arms outstretched toward the earth. Everytime we see a rainbow, we should be reminded of that covenant. We meet underneath our rainbow this morning. The residents of Golden Rain, who don't have any use for words, are with us again. They feel themselves being in a different space. They experience an atmosphere different from the one they are used to, but that's all. They enjoy things intensely, however. Those colors of the rainbow, for instance, which together constitute light, are a symbol of God's love for people.

In addition to the leaders, many parents are also present. Today we celebrate Parents' Day. While participating, each one of them will experience this celebration in his or her own way. They have entrusted their children to our care because they weren't able to take care of them at home any longer. Being forced to give them up has very often caused them pain and grief. We often don't realize how much they have suffered and still may be hurting. Meeting under the rainbow together with their children and those taking care of them will do these parents good. It's comforting to strengthen one another as we put our trust in God, who encompasses the whole world and, with it, all that people may have to go through.

The Liturgy

The chapel is only dimly lit. From the ceiling all kinds of silver strips are hanging, the breeze from a fan moving them. In the background, solemn music resounds. The candles on the altar are burning. The atmosphere is so restful that people can't help but speak in whispers. Beds and wheelchairs are drawn up. Some of the leaders and parents take their disabled children in their laps. Others lay their children down on mattresses near the altar and sit down close beside them. Our residents are remarkably quiet, making only joyful sounds. After bidding everyone welcome, the pastor introduces the celebration: "It's nice being here together this morning. A hearty welcome to all dads and moms who came here to participate in this celebration with us. A very special welcome, too, to the Golden Rain residents." No doubt they will enjoy themselves today. They can be intensely occupied with colors, wind, and music.

Seeing them busy sometimes, one wonders what's going through their minds. This morning we'll try to enter into their world, commending to God their world and ours. And so we make a big sign of the cross and pray: "God our Father, here we are. How wonderful, being allowed to be together with you today—parents and residents, everyone with his or her own color, all of them the way you created them, people to be loved. We want to be here together, because we believe and want to celebrate your loving us, particularly those who are so delicate and vulnerable. God our Father, may this hour do us good. May we always be united with each other and you. Amen."

We play a spotlight on the rainbow. All attention is now focused on it. With soft music in the background, we continue our meditation. Referring to Genesis 9:11-17, we tell about how once the water of misery and destruction has gone down, Noah is on dry ground. Then he sees the rainbow! All the colors, together making up the light, are in it: The *dark blue* of the night, the impenetrable color of anxiety. The *purple* of mourning and grief, for centuries the color of deep compassion. But also in the purple, a little bit of pink shines through. The *red* of the wine with which we celebrate. The *blue* of the sky that sometimes offers us space again. The *yellow* of the light that becomes visible sometimes. Thus, dreaming about all these colors, we are able to attach experiences of life to each one of them.

Using a fluid projector, we begin projecting all kinds of colors on the walls and ceiling. They are reflected by the rustling silver strips, softly moving in the air. It's one big feast of colors. Soft music resounds. Now and then the chirping of birds can be heard. Everybody is fascinated. Everyone wants this to last for a while.

The pastor invites everyone to look at the rainbow again. Meditating, he says: "That's the way the biblical man looked at the rainbow. We can look at it the same way, too. Noah saw the bow in the sky. For him it was a sign that while floating in his ark, God was with him. He has escaped from misery; he can start a new life. Through rain and dampness he sees a new light—a refracting light that becomes a sign of the covenant. God won't let him or his people down. God's rainbow is like a protecting arm reaching from heaven to earth.

"To celebrate that God loves you, to believe that he won't let you down, not even when you are up to your neck in difficulties, to trust that you don't have to drown in your misery, will not always be easy. Perhaps that sign of the rainbow, that sign of God's promise reaching from heaven to earth, may give us some support. And, we will need each other, extending a helping hand to one another."

The light that was playing on the rainbow has been switched off. The play of colors still continues for a while. The music is now getting louder. The whistle of the birds and the gurgle of the water in the background can be heard clearly. It is as if we were at the beach. There is a nice, relaxed atmosphere. The pastor picks up the thread again, and meditating, he continues: "Shouldn't we have to do that more—just lying in the grass and enjoying ourselves? With the sun on our faces, listening to the birds? We know that it is good for us, and yet we don't do it enough. Could that be the reason why Jesus was in the open so often, on the mountain, at the lake to enjoy the blue color of its water, in the green grass, to break the bread? With the yellow grain in his hands, to tell something about it? Don't worry! That's what he wants to tell us. Get out of that busy town. Just enjoy all the beauty that's around you. In his Gospel, Saint Luke mentions something about this [see Luke 12:22-31]. 'Look at the birds in the sky.' " We keep quiet for a moment, so everyone can hear the birds' whistling and chirping. "Look at the flowers."

Now a spotlight is played on a large bed of flowers. A profusion, a wealth of colors and smell. Those residents who are able to walk emerge from the semidarkness and come to the beauty of all these flowers. Standing around them, we look at them and talk about them: "Just look, how beautiful they are! God our Father made them that way—just smell! You know what Jesus says? 'Even though you may put on the nicest clothes, even the ones of King Solomon, you couldn't match their beauty.'

"People differ as much as these flowers do. But God loves each one of us, the way we are, with our own 'color.' Some flowers blossom, others haven't opened up yet and need sun and warmth to burst open. To develop fully, people, too, need the sun and the warmth of others who love them."

Once they have returned to their seats, the pastor concludes the meditation: "Thus, Jesus told us not to work and plod all the time. God our Father knows what we need. Dare we believe this? Our residents serve as an example. Wouldn't it be wonderful just to live and enjoy ourselves the way they do?"

Strumming, the guitar takes over with a song about the happiness that is hidden everywhere. The candles of our prayer candle are lit, and we pray for the children sitting in our laps. We are thankful for the colors, the wind, the music. We are thankful that we may believe that God keeps on loving us, that we may feel his love. Didn't he put his bow in the sky?

We hold a short table service. Most of the residents are preoccupied with whatever has been keeping them busy. They look at the colors and rustle the silver strips that surround them. Some of the parents don't care for this table service; others, however, just like the opportunity to feed themselves right now with the bread of the Lord.

After the celebration someone remarks: ''How wonderful to be able to enjoy yourself so delightfully. You know, for a moment, I started to dream and I almost fell asleep. I was feeling very happy!''

Could that be what Jesus meant?

The celebration has lasted about one hour, but the time has gone quickly. Afterward, we realize that the theme of God's providence could have been used on two Sundays. We could have talked about the way it is expressed by the rainbow on the first Sunday, and on another Sunday about God's providence as it manifests itself in the flowers of the field.

Part IV
Celebrating Life

A Jubilee:
When Flowers Speak

Preparation

This Jubilee is being held on the occasion of the fiftieth anniversary of Huize Ursula, our home for people with mental retardation in Nieuwveen. The elements it contains could be used on other occasions as well, for example, weddings, parish anniversaries, Mother's Day, and other special days.

Celebrating a Jubilee is looking back. Everyone who arrives at such an event brings his or her own memories. There might be a variety of them, ranging from feelings of gratitude and joy for all the happy moments to feelings of discomfort and disappointment for all the trouble and pain that has been endured. In this Jubilee, as we try to do justice to all the feelings of those present, contradictory though they might be, we want to take the "rain and shine" of fifty years at Ursula to the Lord. Nothing better than to have flowers speak. That's why all those who have been invited, as well as the management and residents, have been asked to bring along a flower or a branch. Carefully chosen, these will reveal something about their owner's relationship to this home and his or her feelings on the occasion of this Jubilee. In a collection of flowers and branches, we will then take this whole living reality of fifty years at Ursula to the Lord.

Once we have mailed the invitations, we wonder whether we haven't gone too far. Isn't it unbecoming to give an "assignment" to those we have formally invited—the bishop, the parents? Is it not, all in all, too difficult a task for every one of them, of all times, in January, a month in which it is hard to find any flowers?

At any rate, the response has been both overwhelming and moving. Through the snow they arrive: the bishop, the Sisters who had worked at Ursula, the parents. And sure enough, most of them have brought along a branch or a flower, some of them even a plant. Our own residents have some flowers, too. For them, when there are no flowers, there is no feast. Very quickly, the skillfull hands of our gardeners have arranged all these branches and flowers into a few beautiful bouquets to be used as additional chapel decorations. Thus everyone present appears before the Lord with his or her own flower and color.

The Liturgy

When these bouquets are in place, the service starts. Representatives of the various groups are invited to tell something about the flower or branch they have brought. The branch of the Ursuline Sisters, who founded Huize Ursula, has red berries. One of them explains its meaning: "Thanks to our care and the sense of security we offer, our residents are able to grow. This branch has groups of berries, which symbolize the residents of this home: they, too, are living together in groups. The little leaves bent around them are the assistants. The branch symbolizes the organization, which got its origin from and was rooted in the gospel, when the Sisters accepted their mission fifty years ago."

Next the bishop is asked to present to God in prayer this single, diverse, and living reality that is Huize Ursula, and he does this with great feeling.

Now three of the residents come forward. It is their time now to speak in their own chapel. Each holds a flower, and each tells the story that goes with it: "Flowers go with a feast.

I love to be living here, therefore a rosy rose, because I think it is pretty." "This tulip is mine and Ursula's. I like to live in Ursula just like this new tulip." "A pine branch—look at it carefully; you can see many pine needles. They stand for the residents and the staff. The branch holds them together. That's a sign of solidarity."

After this we read in the Book of God about the lilies in the field: "Think of the flowers, how they grow. They never have to spin or weave. Yet I assure you not even Solomon in all his regalia was robed like one of these" (Luke 12:22-31).

The pastor begins to speak, giving special attention to Ursula's residents. This time, he wants to dwell, together with them, upon this colorful happening—as usual, by way of a dialogue. He begins by reading the text printed in the liturgy booklet. Then he asks, "Are flowers able to speak? Has anyone ever heard one talk?" They roar with laughter: flowers that talk, that's too ridiculous, that is just foolish! The pastor, however, remains undaunted by this first reaction: "When you give your dad or mom a bouquet, then you want to say something, don't you? Why else should you give them flowers?" That they know! From left and right they start answering this question. "We want to make mama happy." "We want to say 'Congratulations,' and 'I think you are nice.'" Thus it becomes clear: although flowers aren't able to talk, they enable us to express certain things.

We look around the chapel. Today it is beautifully decorated. "Do you have any idea how long the gardeners have been working on all these decorations? For at least three days!" A shout of amazement goes up: "That long?" The gardeners are given spontaneous and heartfelt applause. The pastor asks whether they know how much flowers actually cost. There is one who knows: "A bunch of flowers costs five dollars, and that much money only buys ten flowers!" "So you can imagine how much this whole beautiful decoration must have cost!" The pastor takes a bunch of plastic flowers. Showing them, he challenges: "All those flowers in winter—that's foolish and too expensive. We had better take plastic flowers. You don't need to buy new ones every time, and at least these aren't that expensive. And plastic flowers are strong. They won't fall apart. Look at this!" Saying this, the pastor bangs the bunch of plastic flowers against the lectern. Highly indignant, an acolyte stands up. That's really going too far. He heads for the microphone and says: "Don't do that. Stop bashing those flowers!" The pastor picks up the thread again: "Strong plastic flowers—they won't die. You only need to buy them once and that's all. Wouldn't it be better to leave these really expensive flowers in the store from now on?"

The residents grow silent. Then the protest gets going: "Giving flowers is nice, isn't it? You see that your mama is happy. And the real flowers here are nice, too." Thus, we come to discover that it is actually a good thing that real flowers die. That way you can buy new ones every time and say time and again that you love your mother. It's true that real flowers are more expensive than plastic ones. But real love has its price. Jesus said that to a lady who bought a very expensive perfume. When you really love somebody, you don't mind the money. That's why we have all these flowers here to celebrate Ursula. All these efforts and all that love during all these fifty years— that's of a great price, too. We must never allow this home to become a sterile institution. Next, we read for a moment about what Jesus says about flowers: "Think of the flowers, how beautiful they are. . . ." God made them that way. They burst open in the sun. So we, too, thrive when we can bask in the sun of God's care and in the love of one another.

The bishop takes up this line. He has brought a beautiful orchid. It is fragile and vulnerable, and so it stands for all that people have to take care of. What God has entrusted to us often becomes better when seen as part of a larger whole. To illustrate this, the bishop puts his orchid into the large bouquet of flowers he holds in his hands. It symbolizes the whole Huize Ursula community, every resident with his or her own color in that larger whole. The bishop gets a warm applause.

Then we go to the table for the celebration of the Eucharist. After the blessing, the biggest and most beautiful bouquets are given as presents to the parents and the ailing Sisters who have worked at Ursula. In this way, we honor them and show our gratitude. The flowers that are left are arranged in small bouquets and sent to the various sections. A small card attached to each reads: "With these flowers we thank all the people of your section for their great devotion to Huize Ursula."

Some time later we put together a collection of the good wishes and memories from all the cards that were attached to the flowers. All parents and guests who attended the celebration receive one in memory of this service.

A Ceremony of Baptism: Living Water

Preparation

Our residents are fond of water. They like to play with it. For them it is a pleasant experience. The challenge facing our liturgy group in preparing this baptismal celebration is whether we will be able to make the life-giving qualities of the baptismal water understandable for our residents. Eventually, we decide that they themselves should bring the water needed for the baptism. After all, the baby is to be baptized at "our home." Therefore, we, together, ought to make sure there will be enough water to baptize the child. And in this way, the residents, in their own sections, will be able to look forward to the coming Sunday's event.

For our residents, "at our home" means "at our chapel," "belonging to Jesus' friends." The names of those who have been baptized are written in the big register of baptisms. Every time a child is baptized, the pastor tells the residents how many friends have now been added to the list. To highlight the fact that through baptism the baby is going to be a "member" of our family, all the residents join the pastor in pronouncing loudly and solemnly the baptismal formula, beginning with the words "in the name of the Father. . . . " During the week preceding the celebration, a special invitation is sent to all the

residents. It reads like this: "Next Sunday we are going to baptize a little child in the chapel. He is called Ricky. His uncle
is living with us here in our home. Ricky's papa and mama
are very pleased that he will be baptized at our home. Would
all of you be so kind as to bring some water to be used at the
baptism?"

In the sanctuary a well has been placed, made of solid cardboard with a small roof on top and a tackle with which a pail
could be lowered into it. In addition, a large fishbowl, a with-
ered plant, and the baptismal font have been readied. In the
font, a small fountain has been constructed in order to bring
the water "to life" again. The background themes of this baptismal celebration will be water and community. The whole
celebration, actually nothing but an extended baptismal
celebration, will not take more than an hour.

The Liturgy

Shuffling carefully as they carry their bottles, glasses, and
mugs of water, they enter the chapel. Some of them want to
pour the water into the baptismal font immediately. But that's
not the idea, and so we ask them to hold on to it for a while.
In the words of welcome, Ricky's papa and mama are singled
out for greeting. The pastor also points out Ricky's uncle.
Beaming, he gets to his feet and receives a heartfelt applause.

Now we make a sign of the cross. Faithful chapel goers
know that the time in between two signs of the cross is set
aside for God our Father in a very special way. Together we
pray: "God our Father, we are together here to stay with you
for a while. We are pleased to know you are loving us. Today
we enjoy having this little child with us. His name is Ricky.
Together we want to baptize him. Thus he is going to belong
to you, and a little bit to us. Amen."

Then the pastor walks toward the baptismal font. When he
finds it to be completely dry, he asks who has brought some
water along. Bottles, mugs, and glasses are raised enthusiastically. Asked whether they have already used water this morning, shouts can be heard in the chapel: "Taking a shower,"

"Brushing my teeth," "Having tea." Now the fishbowl with live fish and the plant in dire need of water get some attention. After all this commotion, the residents come forward to fill the baptismal font. On the sound equipment Handel's *Water Music* is heard. And as the baptismal font is being filled, the rippling water blends into the murmur of the sea's waves, filling the chapel with the sounds of water. Suddenly, as we sing a festive song about water, the fountain begins spouting. We are singing, so it seems, the water into existence. We listen in silence to the splashing water, and then we pray: "God our Father, we hear running water. Delicious, cool, fresh water. Thank you for the water, in which we may play and wash and which we can drink. Thank you for the water from heaven that makes everything grow, and also for this baptismal water, which we are now going to bless. It will enable us to manifest your love of people, and today, in particular, your love of Ricky. Amen."

The pastor points to the well: "We have a faucet and a shower. That wasn't that way in the days of Jesus. Then, one had to go outside to get water from a well! Our people still remember that cardboard well in the sanctuary. It was once used in a Christmas play." Enthused, someone shouts that the wheel has to be turned! From behind the chapel one of the leaders, disguised as an Oriental woman, walks forward carrying a jar on top of her head. Breathlessly, all the residents watch as she draws water and pours it from the pail into her jar.

Now the moment has come to read and act out the story of the living water (John 4:1-15). The leader plays the role of the Samaritan woman. With the approval of the whole chapel, the pastor is allowed to play the role of Jesus. After a long and tiring journey, "Jesus" arrives at the well, thirsty and dusty. And there he gets into conversation with the woman. When she tells him that she is a foreigner and for that reason poorly thought of, a wave of indignation passes through the chapel. Very slowly, the pastor, in his role as Jesus, starts drinking the water that the woman has drawn from the well especially for him. As if mesmerized, the residents "drink" with him. The pastor makes known that this mug of water has done him a lot of good by saying, ''That water will do me all the good in the world! I feel like a new creature. I wish I could be living water for other people, too, so that they in turn might become fresh and new again!''

Now four residents step forward from the chapel to drink some of the water, too. Using the microphone, they let everyone know how delicious it is. ''Whoever gives a cup of cold water to these little ones . . . ''

The Samaritan woman wants to wash Jesus' hands, too. The water she pours runs all over the floor. But so what? Her headcloth serves as a towel. From such refreshing and living water, we want to have some for the baptism. Solemnly, water is drawn from the well and added to the baptismal water. Now everything is ready.

The uncle goes to get the baby to be baptized. Proudly he carries him in procession into the chapel, led by the nephews and nieces carrying their baptismal candles. Ricky is warmly welcomed with a song: ''Come in and tell us your name. . . .'' Under way, he gets quite a few gentle strokes.

After Ricky's parents have pronounced their baptismal vows, Ricky's father writes his son's name in the register of baptisms. The pastor announces that there are now seventy-five names in it. Applause is the spontaneous reaction. When the moment of the actual baptism arrives, everyone stands up. Some draw closer so as not to miss a thing. As soon as the pastor starts pronouncing the formula: ''In the name of the Father . . . ,'' all help by joining in. After the baptismal ceremony there is clearly some bustle and joy, and we express that joy in a song, because from now on this child will be one of ours.

Before proceeding to the anointing, the pastor has the residents ''test'' the oil. They inspect it, to make sure it's all right. After all, one should be able to smell that the baby has been baptized recently. The baptismal candle is lit from the narrative one, the Easter candle—all children who are baptized should radiate something of Jesus' light. We pray the Our Father, because this child, being baptized, now belongs to the family of God our Father. Finally, we sing ''For he's a jolly good fellow.'' Almost everyone comes forward to congratulate Ricky's papa and mama and, of course, his uncle, who is standing close by, beaming. For Ricky, there are drawings and also a handmade doll.

A Ceremony of Confirmation:
God Our Father Looks at the Heart

A Question to Begin With

Does the administration of the sacrament of confirmation to our residents make any sense? That is a question that we pastors have been grappling with for a long time. In an ordinary parish, youngsters who want to be confirmed are presumed to have made a more-or-less conscious choice for the Church in which they were baptized and the faith in which they have been raised. With regard to our residents, that kind of a choice is out of the question. Our residents rarely make choices, nor could they in this case. Their whole life, after all, is determined and guided by others.

But people with mental retardation have a right to learn to know God. They, too, believe, and they do so in their own way. Their childlike receptivity of God our Father is often moving. As a case in point, they will never start anything they consider important without saying a prayer first. The sacrament of confirmation knows of no exceptions. It enables all Christians, able in body and mind or not, to become people loving each other in Jesus' Spirit. Expressions such as "to be kind like Jesus," "to share," "to make up for something," "to give another person a new chance," are obvious manifestations of authentic Christian values and the activities of the Spirit. By and large, they feel very much at home in the whole world of religious expressions of our faith, and they love to join in. Training and confirming them means giving their way of believing a place within our community of the Church. They are entitled to this. After all, we accepted this responsibility for them when they were baptized and received into the community of our faith.

Is the Bishop Himself Coming?

The parents and the attendants are involved in the preparation. On one of the parents' evenings, one of the mothers asks whether the bishop will come to confirm their children himself. In her question a lot of emotions can be heard. Very often, parents have been through a lot with their children. Perhaps they have had to wage a bitter struggle with God to find the right way for their handicapped child. All of a sudden we realize that this sacrament of confirmation will also confirm these parents in their care for their children, that they also will benefit.

Preparation

For several reasons the story of David's election to become king seems to be an excellent starting point. In preparing the celebration of confirmation we will give this story due attention. David was only a weak little fellow. Nobody considered him eligible to be anointed king. So he had to be called from the field. God had told Samuel not to trust appearances: "For people look at the appearance, I, however, look at the heart" (1 Sam 16:7). Our homes, too, are often built outside, in the field. Like David, we have to call our people and then anoint them with sweet-smelling oil. When someone gives you something that smells pleasant, it means that that person loves you.

A number of pictures, made into a coloring book, are used for the religious instruction of our residents. These books are to be ready three days before the celebration. The reason: The bishop himself will "check" whether they have done a good job. During the Ascension Day celebration (three days before confirmation) the books are wrapped up and sent to the bishop.

That in itself is quite a ceremony. Four or five residents lend a hand and put the postage stamps on the package. If the "homework" has been done well, the bishop will set his seal on it: the seal of the diocese and his signature! All the residents have worked on the coloring books to the best of their ability. Some of the books are full of scratches, others have been worked at with great precision. Obviously, in all the fervor, the color couldn't always be kept within the lines. The bishop will be treated to quite a colorful happening!

The Liturgy

At the beginning of the celebration, all those to be confirmed receive a corsage. The color of the flower determines the sequence in which they will be called by the bishop. Immediately, all are in a festive mood.

At the entrance procession, the exercise books are solemnly carried into the chapel. These are placed in the center next to a big horn like the one Samuel uses in the story in the Book of God. The aroma of the oil surrounds them. That has been carefully provided for, because our residents will have to spread Christ's good smell. The celebration elaborates on this idea, which we have talked about in our preparation.

David's story is told once more. Then, appropriately, the exercise books become the bishop's sermon. All he has to do is leaf through the pages and select those residents in particular who need some extra confirmation. In looking at the books, the bishop applies very special criteria. After all, God said to Samuel, "Don't trust appearances, but look at the heart!" Although some of the books are full of scratches, the fact that they have worked on them with all their heart deserves appreciation. That's why each book has been signed by the bishop and marked with the seal of the diocese. As we light the seven candles representing the seven gifts of Jesus' Spirit on our prayer candle stand, we pray that we might receive the good Spirit of Jesus. After this, using the beautiful big horn, the bishop proceeds with the anointing. The parents escort their child to be confirmed, introduce him or her to the bishop, and tell him something about the particular way of believing of their candidate: "Our John loves God our Father very much!" "Ria likes to go to the chapel." "Our Joke doesn't know much about God. Yet we are convinced he loves her anyway."

Here and there, some emotion among the parents is noticeable. But those children who have been confirmed are all very happy. Some of them give the bishop a heartening tap back on the shoulder. After the anointing the exercise books are returned to the residents. In addition, all receive a picture of the bishop to be put into it. A little cross, a present from the bishop, is put around each child's neck. It makes them very happy, because everything with a cross on it belongs to God our Father. So wearing a cross around your neck shows you are a child of God.

After the administration of confirmation, we celebrate Holy Mass. At the distribution of Communion all those confirmed step forward, keeping a tight grip on their exercise books. Not for all the world would they want to lose them.

After the celebration, the bishop receives numerous drawings and even a homemade painting.

God Chooses Whom He Wants

"A long time ago, as many as three thousand years, there lived a king in the land of Israel. His name was Saul. He disobeyed the Lord. God wanted a new king, one who would be more obedient.

"So one day God told Samuel, a priest, 'Go to Bethlehem to a farmer by the name of Jesse. I am going to make one of his sons king. Anoint him so he will smell sweet. That way everyone will know that I love him and that he is allowed to be king.

"Samuel was in charge of the temple, the house of God. He took a horn filled with fragrant oil and set out on the journey.

"Jesse, the farmer, was very pleased with Samuel's visit. 'Just call your sons in,' said Samuel. There they came, the eldest in front. He was a sturdy fellow, so Samuel thought, 'No doubt, it will be he.' But God gave Samuel a warning. Deep down in his heart, he heard God's voice saying, 'Beware, Samuel, of whom you are going to choose. The question is not whether somebody is big or strong or good looking! God doesn't look in the same way people do. They often judge by appearances. In God's eyes being a good person, being willing to follow orders, is what is important. God looks at the heart!'

"When Jesse's sons were all at table, Samuel took a good look at all of them. In his heart he sensed that none of these sons would become king. 'Strange,' he thought. 'After all, God has told me that it would be one of Jesse's sons. What about that?'

" 'Are these really all your sons?' Samuel asked the farmer. 'No,' he replied, 'the youngest is not among them. He is tending sheep. He isn't strong, and also he is much too small, but he is all right tending sheep. His name is David.'

"The brothers sneered. 'David, king? It's enough to make a cat laugh!' But Samuel said, 'Call David. I want to see him!' David came home as fast as he could to appear before Samuel. He gasped for breath with running. His face was red, and his shoes were still covered with mud. Samuel looked at little David with his head of red hair. Suddenly he knew for certain, this was to be the new king.

"Samuel stood up and went to David and poured sweet-smelling oil over his head. The whole house was filled with its fragrance. Samuel said to David, 'God loves you very much. You are good at heart. That's why I anoint you—so all people will know you are going to be the king. I hope you'll be a good one.'

"That's the way God elected David to be king. The brothers simply didn't understand. They were green with jealousy.

"That's the way God is. He looks at the heart.

"David was very glad to know that God loved him. He tried

to be extra obedient. People noticed that something special had happened to David. It looked as if God had given him new strength.''

(Freely rendered from 1 Sam 16)

An Anointing of the Sick: Don't Let Him Down

Within our Roman Catholic tradition we experience the anointing of the sick as a sacrament. Not too long ago, this sacrament was often postponed until the very last moment so that all sins could be purged and preparations made to meet God. However, the fact that a person is seriously ill is reason enough for friends to give support by being near; and indeed, the value of this kind of support is being recognized more and more. One in faith, we are able to commend his or her critical situation to God. The intentions of our prayers are always adjusted to the patient's actual situation. Sometimes we ask for recovery; at other times, we pray for God's strength and merciful love.

Does it make sense to anoint children? Have they already committed sin that has to be healed? As the Letter of James tells us (5:14-15), by administering the sacrament of the sick to children we express our feelings of care, love, involvement, and solidarity. Particularly when we are exposed to the plight of children and the mentally handicapped, we are battered by all kinds of emotions—rebelliousness, anger, concern. We can be freed of these feelings when we pray for, encourage, or, as Saint James suggests, anoint the sick.

Preparation

We feel that it is very important to involve the parish itself whenever the pastor of our congregation is called upon to see a seriously ill parishioner. Together with staff and family, we try to present to God this difficult stage of life and all the questions it evokes, for these critical situations put one's faith in God to the test and turn it into an inner conflict. Preparing ourselves together for the celebration around the sick results in having more time and space for our own questions. The preparation itself turns out to be a liberating experience, so much so that, prepared in this way, everyone in the community wants to be present at an anointing.

The Liturgy

Antoon is in the hospital for a serious spine operation. He suffers a lot and is not doing well at all. Together with his mother, brother, and all the attendants, we go and see him. Now that he is having a hard time, we want to be near him. Antoon is surprised seeing all these well-known faces surrounding him. He is also a bit nervous. We have brought along from the chapel the Book of God our Father. Carrying the book in his hands, the pastor asks Antoon, "Do you know why all of us came to see you?" Antoon looks around, wondering. He doesn't know what to answer. The pastor explains: "We have been reading in the Book of God our Father and it says: 'If any one of you is ill and is suffering agonies, don't let him down. You have to go and see him so that he doesn't feel lonesome. And you must pray together that he may not suffer too much. Lay your hands on him. This way he feels that you won't let him down.' That's the reason why we are here. Look and see who came to see you."

Antoon looks around the circle. We speak the names of all the attendants, and each one of them smiles or says a word of friendship. Sometimes someone whispers a little secret to Antoon into his ear—something they alone know. There is some emotion and yet, at the same time, a relaxed, comfortable feeling. "So we have come here to pray together for you," the pastor says. "I have also brought along oil to make a sign of the cross with it, for God our Father belongs here, too. He has to take good care of you. After all, you are his child!"

Antoon wants to get a smell of the oil first, just the way we always do at baptism. He sniffs. This oil doesn't smell as pleasant as the oil of baptism. This oil is, after all, for sick people, the pastor explains. It is meant to help us ask God our Father for healing. After this explanation, Antoon has no objection to being anointed by the pastor. We ask God to support Antoon, who is suffering so much pain. We ask for his recovery, if that is possible. His mother gives him a little cross, just the way she used to every night before he went to bed, and also a kiss. We hold each other's hands and pray: "God our Father, here we are all together. We love Antoon and we won't let him down. Help us to take good care of him. We ask you to do the same. Amen."

Before receiving Holy Communion together with Antoon, we say, as children of the same Father, the prayer Jesus taught us. After the service, Antoon is given a bouquet of flowers as a remembrance of our visit. Then we decide who, in turn, will stay with him. Having someone in his room all the time makes Antoon feel more at ease.

In spite of our feelings of anxiety and grief, we go home with a sense of satisfaction. In the liturgy service we have become aware once again that Antoon has been entrusted to our care and that together we have to live up to our duty: to take care of him. During this service we have shared our faith and hope. If Antoon should leave us through this illness, we are convinced he'll be in the good hands of God.

Saying Farewell:
"In heaven there is
never a thunderstorm"

Tom died suddenly. Only a few days ago he had come out of the hospital. We had welcomed him with a big bunch of flowers. Now all of a sudden, he is dead. Everyone is dismayed. Soundlessly and solemnly, the whole community sits together. The pastor and most of the group leaders are with them; the other ones are preparing Tom for the funeral. There isn't much need for talk, but they want to know whether Tom's father and mother know it already and whether they have come. They also want to know when the funeral will be held. They are told that Tom's body is being washed right now. Once the group leaders have finished that, he'll get on his Sunday best.

As soon as Tom is ready, they want to see him. Together they stand around the bier. Piet puts yesterday's welcome flowers next to it. We say hello to Tom. We pray for him and for everyone in distress. We pray, too, for ourselves. We stay together a long time that evening. Even in those long silent moments, we have much to share.

Sunday Morning
We come together for our regular weekly liturgy service. In addition to Tom's fellow patients, the group leaders and

a welfare worker are present. Jaap brings his statue of the Good Shepherd along and puts it on the altar table. Geert does the same with a picture of Tom. Jos takes care of some decorations. On his way to the chapel he gathered some cuckoo flowers. Ties carries their ward's Easter candle along.

All the items standing there together on the altar table tell today's story: the story of Tom and his Good Shepherd. Tom's fellow residents mention that Tom has had quite a few "good shepherds"—his father and mother, his group leader, Liesbeth, but also his friend Jaap. Ever since Tom came home, Jaap sat by his bed and always walked with him when he had to go to the restroom. Together, these "shepherds" can tell a lot about Tom: how he was and what he did. Peter says that Tom often called him *Pieter de stier* (Peter the bull), a take-off on his last name. Actually he could not stand Tom's needling, but now, remembering what has happened, tears appear in his eyes. "Now he never will say that again," he says. Huub remembers how afraid Tom was of thunderstorms and of quarrels. "In heaven there is never a thunderstorm!" he concludes reassuringly. When each person's tale has been finished and they have all stopped crying, we light the small home Easter candle, our story candle about Tom and Jesus. We commend Tom to his Good Shepherd in heaven. Singing a song, we ask for support and strength for his father and mother and also for ourselves.

Next to the Good Shepherd statue and Tom's picture, we put the bread and the wine. Since Tom has died with Jesus, he'll also rise with him. That's what Jesus promised on Holy Thursday.

We go to Communion after the Our Father and a short preparatory prayer. Then, in a prayer at the end of the service, the pastor thanks God for the coresidents' and guides' loving care and friendship for Tom, and he asks God's blessing for all of them. Finally, the Good Shepherd statue, Tom's picture, and the candle are returned to their owners. The pastor suggests that the home Easter candle be lighted every time they are talking about Tom—during coffee breaks or meals.

When everyone goes home, the pastor and the social worker join Jos, Geert, and the others to have a cup of coffee with them. Just like in the chapel, statue, picture, and lighted candle are put on the coffee table.

The Meantime

The two days preceding the funeral are very valuable. They are very much needed to enable us to share our despair and grief with one another and to be one another's support. Crying is not a shame. There is, however, also a lot of laughter, particularly when amusing stories about Tom are remembered. In those two days the texts are "born" by which we will commemorate Tom. A group leader writes a poem about him, and some of the residents compose short prayers, which they want to recite during the service all by themselves. Together, they also decide to see Tom to his last resting place. They are going to attach yellow and white ribbons to the casket, which they are going to hold while walking along in the cortege. Yellow and white were Tom's favorite colors.

For a moment, a kind of argument threatens. It had been agreed that all of them would put on their Sunday best. But Henk refuses, and the others don't like that decision at all. Finally, Henk loses his temper and runs into his room. After a lot of patient questioning it becomes clear what is bothering him. In about two days Henk will be going to a wedding. Wearing the same suit both at the funeral and at the wedding feast would be impossible! Together we select some other nice clothes for Henk to wear at the funeral.

The Funeral

Everyone is ready for this last farewell. The chapel is packed. We celebrate Tom's funeral not only with residents and their guides but also with family and former neighbors on the street where Tom lived before. On the altar, we have placed once again the Good Shepherd statue, Tom's picture, and the "story candle." Next to the altar, the Easter candle burns. There is a decoration made of yellow and white flowers. Everyone settles around the casket, which is standing in front of the altar.

The pastor tells them about the Good Shepherd and how many have been good shepherds to Tom. Jaap mentions once more these "good shepherds" who have come together to commemorate Tom: his father and mother, Lenie, Dorien, the other group leaders. Seeing tears in their eyes, he starts crying himself. Ties, the altar boy, pulls him onto a chair next to him and tries to cheer him up. Thus Jaap has also found his good shepherd. Dorien starts reading out loud the poem she composed about Tom. One by one, all the residents and their leaders put a flower on the casket. It's becoming a colorful bouquet, as colorful as Tom was himself. Theo has made two drawings. One of them is of an opened drawbridge and a boat. On the vessel, a prayer: "There is the steamboat coming. It's taking Tom to heaven to be with the angels. God our Father takes care of him. Amen." Theo puts this drawing on the casket. He gives the other one to Tom's parents. Then Peter reads his prayer and puts the text on the casket. The same is done by Ties and Johan.

Once more the pastor says that Jesus remains a Good Shepherd to Tom, even though he has passed away. In a prayer, we thank God our Father for all those pastoral cares Tom enjoyed. The bread and the wine are put on the altar. The Communion prayer follows. After that, the liturgical "farewell prayer" is said. The casket is sprinkled with holy water and incensed. Then Tom's brother prays and commemorates him. We sing his favorite song. Tom's brothers and sisters carry him to the hearse.

Burial

On their way to the grave Tom's coresidents walk alongside the casket, each holding a ribbon attached to it. After reaching the gravesite, the casket is lowered and the funeral prayers are said. In parting everyone strews some soil on it, saying, "Farewell, Tom."

After the funeral we meet again to have some coffee and eat some buns together. We agree to meet again after three months. Then we'll tell each other how we have fared since Tom passed away.

Afterword

Creating structure in communicating and educating people with mental retardation is from an orthopedagogic point of view a right position and one of paramount importance. Because of limited intellectual faculties, people with mental retardation are not, or are only partially, able to bring structure into their lives. They aren't able, therefore, to take part in a world that is by and large geared toward verbal and intellectual communication. In situations in which spoken language counts for little, it will be necessary to find alternatives for mutual communication. That is why in the last few years the principle of total communication in treating people with mental retardation has gained increasing acceptance. Structure is making, according to each one's needs, the lives of brain-damaged people clearer, more understandable, more predictable, and therefore safer. If we are prepared to use forms of communication other than verbal, conditions for improved communications will be created. This way, there will be more room for safety, mutual trust, and a sense of security. In a word, structure and the ability to communicate set the framework for human encounter. The latter is a necessary condition for the development of human relations and for making them actively as well as passively more meaningful.

From their engagement with people with mental retardation, the authors of this collection have made well-thought-out efforts to translate these principles into liturgy celebrations with brain-damaged people. Structure-rendering elements such as feasts, biblical stories, rites, and symbols are conducive to the residents, and we with them, being able to master a common language that emphasizes our equality and enables them, if only for a moment, to transcend their awareness of being disabled.

Very significant is the cyclical character of the liturgical year. The liturgy contributes preeminently by structuring and adding meaning to the many, often confusing experiences that people with mental retardation suffer from. Religious stories or rites are able either to put new meaning on events within a community or to derive meaning from these events themselves, for instance, an anniversary, a farewell, a death. Liturgy celebrated in this way is not something "exclusive," just for that little hour on Sunday morning, but becomes an essential part of everyday life.

Liturgy celebrated this way presupposes, however, that nurses, parents, family, and assistants are and remain constantly informed about it. The quality of the liturgical celebrations described in this collection was obtained because elements creating structure were applied, structures that enabled each participant to portray his or her own story in his or her own manner and in a way others could identify with. They are examples of conditions by which the lives of our fellow human beings with mental retardation can be made more and more valuable.

A. de Johgh
Pedagogue